F. Anstey

Mister Punch's Model Music-Hall Songs and Dramas

Vol. 1

F. Anstey

Mister Punch's Model Music-Hall Songs and Dramas
Vol. 1

ISBN/EAN: 9783337335014

Printed in Europe, USA, Canada, Australia, Japan

Cover: Foto ©Thomas Meinert / pixelio.de

More available books at **www.hansebooks.com**

MR. PUNCH'S

MODEL MUSIC-HALL

SONGS AND DRAMAS

COLLECTED, IMPROVED, AND RE-ARRANGED FROM
"PUNCH"

BY

F. ANSTEY

AUTHOR OF

"THE TINTED VENUS," "VICE VERSA," "A FALLEN IDOL,"
"THE GIANT'S ROBE," ETC.

NEW YORK

NATIONAL BOOK COMPANY

3, 4, 5 AND 6 MISSION PLACE

CONTENTS

6 CONTENTS.

MODEL MUSIC HALL.

INTRODUCTION.

INTRODUCTION.

THE day is approaching, and may even now be within measurable distance, when the Music Halls of the Metropolis will find themselves under yet more stringent supervision than is already exercised by those active and intelligent guardians of middle-class morality, the London County Council. The moral microscope which detected latent indecency in the pursuit of a butterfly by a marionette is to be provided with larger powers, and a still more extended field. In other words, our far-sighted and vigilant County Councilmen, perceiving the futility of delaying the inspection of Variety Entertainments until such improprieties as are contained therein have been suffered to contaminate the public mind for a considerable period, are determined to nip these poison-flowers in the bud for the future; and, unless Mr. Punch is misinformed, will apply to Parliament at the earliest opportunity for clauses enabling them to require each item in every forthcoming performance to be previously submitted to a special committee for sanction and approval.

The conscientious rigor with which they will discharge this new and congenial duty, may perhaps be better understood after perusing the little prophetic sketch which follows; for Mr. Punch's Poet, when not employed in metrical composition, is a Seer of some pretensions in a small way, and several of his predictions have already been shamelessly plagiarized by the unscrupulous hand of Destiny. It is not improbable that this latest effort of his will receive a similar compliment, although this would be more gratifying if Destiny ever condescended to acknowledge such obligations. However, here is the forecast for what it is worth, a sum of incalculable amount : —

POETIC LICENSES.

A VISION OF THE NEAR FUTURE.

SCENE. — *A committee-room of the L. C. C.; Sub-Committee of Censors (appointed, under new regulations, to report on all songs intended to be sung on the Music-Hall Stage), discovered in session.*

MR. WHEEDLER (*retained for the ballad-writers*). The next license I have to apply for is for — well (*with some hesitation*), — a composition which certainly borders on th—er—amorous; but I think, sir, you will allow that it is treated in a purely pastoral and Arcadian spirit.

THE CHAIRMAN (*gravely*). There *are* arcades, Mr. Wheedler, I may remind you, which are by no means pastoral. I cannot too often repeat that we are here to fulfil the mission intrusted to us by the Democracy, which will no longer tolerate in its entertainments anything that is either vulgar, silly, or offensive in the slightest degree.

[*Applause.*

MR. WHEEDLER. Quite so. With your permission, sir, I will read you the ballad.

[*Reads.*

"MOLLY AND I.

" Oh! the day shall be marked in red letter "—
THE CHAIRMAN. One moment, Mr. Wheedler (*conferring with his colleagues*). "Marked with red letter" — isn't that a little — eh? liable to — You don't think they'll have read Hawthorne's book? Very well, then. Go on, Mr. Wheedler, please.

Mr. W. " 'Twas warm, with a heaven so blue."
FIRST CENSOR. Can't pass those two epithets

—you must tone them down, Mr. Wheedler — *much* too suggestive!

MR. W.   That shall be done.

THE CHAIRMAN.   And it ought to be "sky."

MR. W.   " When amid the lush meadows I met her,
                My Molly, so modest and true ! "

SECOND CENSOR.   I object to the word "lush" — a direct incitement to intemperance!

MR. W.   I'll strike it out.   (*Reads.*)

    " Around us the little kids rollicked,
        Light-hearted were all the young lambs —

SECOND CENSOR.   Surely "kids" is *rather* a vulgar expression, Mr. Wheedler ?   Make it "*children*," and I've no objection.

MR. W.   I have made it so.   (*Reads.*)

    " They kicked up their legs as they frolicked " —

THIRD CENSOR.   If that is intended to be done on the stage, I protest most strongly — a highly indecorous exhibition !   [*Murmurs of approval.*

MR. W.   But they're only lambs !

THIRD CENSOR.   Lambs, indeed !   We are determined to put down *all* kicking in Music-hall songs, no matter *who* does it !   Strike that line out.

Mr. W. (*reading*). "And frisked by the side of their dams."

First Censor (*severely*). No profanity, Mr. Wheedler, *if* you please!

Mr. W. Er — I'll read you the refrain. (*Reads, limply.*)

"Molly and I. With nobody nigh.
Hearts all a-throb with a rapturous bliss.
Molly was shy. And (at first) so was I,
Till I summoned up courage to ask for a kiss!"

The Chairman. "Nobody nigh," Mr. Wheedler? I don't quite like that. The Music Hall ought to set a good example to young persons. "Molly and I — *with her chaperon by*," is better.

Second Censor. And that last line — "asking for a kiss" — does the song state that they were formally engaged, Mr. Wheedler?

Mr. W. I — I believe it omits to mention the fact. But (*ingenuously*), it does not appear that the request was complied with.

Second Censor. No matter — it should never had been made. Have the goodness to alter that into — well, something of this kind. "And I always addressed her politely as " Miss." Then we *may* pass it.

MR. W. (*reading the next verse*).

> "She wore but a simple sun-bonnet."

FIRST CENSOR (*shocked*).   Now really, Mr. Wheedler, *really*, sir!

MR. W.   " For Molly goes plainly attired."

FIRST CENSOR (*indignantly*).   I should think so — *Scandalous!*

MR. W.   " Malediction I muttered upon it,
>   One glimpse of her face I desired."

THE CHAIRMAN.   I think my colleague's exception is perhaps just a *leetle* far-fetched.   At all events, if we substitute for the last couplet, —

> " Her dress is sufficient — though on it
> She only spends what is strictly required."

Eh, Mr. Wheedler?   Then we work in a moral as well, you see, and avoid malediction, which can only mean bad language.

MR. W. (*doubtfully*).   With all respect, I submit that it doesn't scan quite so well —

THE CHAIRMAN (*sharply*).   *I* venture to think scansion may be sacrificed to propriety, *occasionally*, Mr. Wheedler — but pray go on.

Mr. W. (*continuing*).

> " To a streamlet we rambled together,
>   I carried her tenderly o'er.
> In my arms — she's as light as a feather —
>   That sweetest of burdens I bore!"

First Censor. I really *must* protest. No properly conducted young woman would ever have permitted such a thing. You must alter that, Mr. Wheedler!

Second C. And I don't know — but I rather fancy there's a " double-intender " in that word " light " — (*to colleague*) — It strikes me — eh ? — what do *you* think?

The Chairman (*in a conciliatory manner*). I am inclined to agree to some extent — not that I consider the words particularly objectionable in themselves, but we are men of the world, Mr. Wheedler, and as such we cannot shut our eyes to the fact that a Music-hall audience is only too apt to find significance in many apparently innocent expressions and phrases.

Mr. W. But, sir, I understood from your remarks recently that the Democracy were strongly opposed to anything in the nature of suggestiveness!

THE CH.   Exactly so; and therefore we cannot allow their susceptibilities to be shocked.   (*With a severe jocosity.*)   Molly and you, Mr. Wheedler, must either ford the stream like ordinary persons, or stay where you are.

MR. W. (*depressed*).   I may as well read the last verse, I suppose : —

> " Then under the flickering willow
>   I lay by the rivulet's brink,
>   With her lap for a sumptuous pillow " —

FIRST CENSOR.   We can't have that.   It is really *not* respectable.

THE CH. (*pleasantly*).   Can't we alter it slightly? " I'd brought a small portable pillow."   No objection to *that!*

[*The other Censors express dissent in undertones.*]

MR. W.   " Till I owned that I longed for a drink."

THIRD C.   No, no!   " A drink! "   We all know what *that* means — alcoholic stimulant of some kind.   At all events that's how the audience are certain to take it.

MR. W. (*feebly*).

> " So Molly her pretty hands hollowed
>   Into curves like an exquisite cup,
>   And draughts so delicious I swallowed,
>   That rivulet nearly dried up ! "

THIRD C. Well, Mr. Wheedler, you're not going to defend *that*, I hope?

MR. W. I'm not prepared to deny that it is silly — *very* silly — but hardly — er — vulgar, I should have thought?

THIRD C. That is a question of taste, which we won't dispute. *I* call it *distinctly* vulgar. Why can't he drink out of his *own* hands?

THE CH. (*blandly*). Allow me. How would *this* do for the second line? " She had a collapsible cup." A good many people *do* carry them. I have one myself. Is that all of your ballad, Mr. Wheedler?

MR. W. (*with great relief*). That *is* all, sir.

[*Censors withdraw, to consider the question.*

THE CH. (*after consultation with colleagues*). We have carefully considered this song, and we are all reluctantly of opinion that we cannot, consistently with our duty, recommend the Council to license it — even with the alterations my colleagues and myself have gone somewhat out of our way to suggest. The whole subject is too dangerous for a hall in which young persons of both sexes are likely to be found assembled; and the absence of any distinct assertion that the young couple — Molly and — ah — the gentleman who narrates the experience — are betrothed, or that their attachment is in any way sanctioned by their parents or guardians, is quite fatal. If we have another ballad of a similar character from the same quarter, Mr. Wheedler, I feel bound to warn you that we may possibly consider it necessary to advise that the poet's license should be cancelled altogether.

Mr. W.   I will take care to mention it to my client, sir.   I understand it is his intention to confine himself to writing Gayety burlesques in future.

The Ch.   A very laudable resolution!   I hope he will keep it.   [*Scene closes in.*

It is hardly possible that any Music-hall Manager or vocalist, irreproachable as he may hitherto have considered himself, can have taken this glimpse into a not very remote futurity without symptoms of uneasiness, if not of positive dismay. He will reflect that the ballad of "Molly and I," however reprehensible it may appear in the fierce light of an L. C. C. Committee Room, is innocuous, and even moral, compared to the ditties in his own *répertoire*.   How, then, can he hope, when his hour of trial strikes, to confront the ordeal with an unruffled shirt-front, or a collar that shall retain the inflexibility of conscious innocence? And he will wish then that he had confined himself to the effusions of a bard who could not be blamed by the most censorious moralist.

Here, if he will only accept the warning in time, is his best safeguard. He has only to buy this little volume, and inform his inquisitors that the songs and business with which he proposes to entertain an ingenuous public are derived from the immaculate pages of Mr. Punch. Whereupon censure will be instantly disarmed, and criticism give place to congratulation. It is just possible, to be sure, that this somewhat confident prediction smacks rather of the poet than the seer, and that even the entertainment supplied by Mr. Punch's Music Hall may, to the purist's eye, present features as suggestive as a horrid vulgar clown, or as shocking as a butterfly, an insect notorious for its frivolity. But then, so might the "songs and business" of the performing canary, or the innocent sprightliness of the educated flea, with its superfluity of legs, all absolutely unclad. At all events, the compiler of this collection ventures to hope that, whether it is fortunate enough to find favor or not with Music-hall "artistes," literary critics, and London County Councilmen,

it contains nothing particularly objectionable to
the rest of the British public. And very likely,
even in this modest aspiration, he is over-sanguine,
and his little joke will be taken seriously. Earn-
estness is so alarmingly on the increase in these
days.

MODEL MUSIC HALL.

SONGS.

1.—THE PATRIOTIC.

THIS stirring ditty—so thoroughly sound and practical under all its sentiment—has been specially designed to harmonize with the recently altered tone of Music-hall audiences, in which a spirit of enlightened Radicalism is at last happily discernible. It is hoped that, both in rhyme and metre, the verses will satisfy the requirements of this most elegant form of composition. The song is intended to be shouted through music in the usual manner by a singer in evening dress, who should carry a small Union Jack carelessly thrust inside his waistcoat. The title is short but taking : —

ON THE CHEAP!

First Verse.

OF a Navy insufficient cowards croak, deah
    boys!
If our place among the nations we're to keep.
But with British beef, and beer, and hearts of oak,
    deah boys! —
(*With enthusiasm.*) We can make a shift to do it
    — On the Cheap!

23

Chorus.

(*With a common-sense air.*)   Let us keep, deah
        boys !   On the Cheap,
While Britannia is the boss upon the deep.
She can wollop an invader, when he comes in his
        Armada,
If she's let alone to do it — On the Cheap !

Second Verse.

(*Affectionately.*)   Johnny Bull is just as plucky as
        he *was*, deah boys !
(*With a knowing wink.*)   And he's wide awake —
        no error !— not asleep ;
But he won't stump up for ironclads — becos, deah
        boys !
He don't see his way to get 'em — On the Cheap !

Chorus.

So keep, deah boys !   On the Cheap,
(*Gallantly.*)   And we'll chance what may hap-
        pen on the deep !
For we can't be the losers if we save the cost o'
        cruisers,
And contentedly continue — On the Cheap !

Third Verse.

The British Isles are not the Conti-nong, deah
 boys!
(*Scornfully.*) Where the Johnnies on defences
 spend a heap.
No! we're Britons, and we're game to jog along,
 deah boys!
(*With pathos.*) In the old time-honored fashion
 — On the Cheap!

Chorus.

(*Imploringly.*) Ah keep, deah boys! On the
 Cheap ;
For the price we're asked to pay is pretty steep.
Let us all unite to dock it, keep the money in our
 pocket,
And we'll conquer or we'll perish — On the
 Cheap!

Fourth Verse.

If the Tories have the cheek to touch our purse,
 deah boys!
Their reward at the elections let 'em reap!
They will find a big Conservative reverse, deah
 boys!
If they can't defend the country — On the Cheap!

Chorus.

They must keep, deah boys! On the Cheap,
Or the lot out of office we will sweep!
Bull gets rusty when you tax him, and his patriotic
    maxim
Is, "I'll trouble you to govern — On the Cheap!"

Fifth Verse (this to be sung shrewdly).

If the gover'ment ain't mugs they'll take the tip,
    deah boys!
Just to look a bit ahead before they leap,
And instead of laying down an extry ship, deah
    boys!
They'll cut down the whole caboodle — On the
    Cheap!

Chorus (with spirit and fervor).

And keep, deah boys! On the Cheap!
For we ain't like a bloomin' lot o' sheep.
When we want to "parry bellum," [1]
            [*Union Jack to be waved here.*
You may bet yer boots we'll tell 'em!
But we'll have the "bellum" "parried" — On the
    Cheap!

---

[1] Music-hall Latinity — "*Para Bellum.*"

This song, if sung with any spirit, should, *Mr. Punch* thinks, cause a positive *furore* in any truly patriotic gathering, and possibly go some way towards influencing the decision of the country, and consequently the fate of the empire, in the next general elections. In the meantime it is at the service of any Champion Music Hall Comique who is capable of appreciating it.

II. — THE TOPICAL-POLITICAL.

IN most respects, no doubt, the present example can boast no superiority to ditties in the same style now commanding the ear of the public. One merit, however, its author does claim for it. Though it deals with most of the burning questions of the hour, it can be sung anywhere with absolute security. This is due to a simple but ingenious method by which the political sentiment has been arranged on the reversible principle. A little alteration here and there will put the singer in close touch with an audience of almost any shade of politics. Should it happen that the title has been already anticipated, *Mr. Punch* begs to explain that the remainder of this sparkling composition is entirely .original ; any similarity with previous works must be put down entirely to " literary coincidence." Whether the title is new or not, it is a very nice one, viz. : —

BETWEEN YOU AND ME — AND THE POST.

(To be sung in a raucous voice, and with a confidential air.)

I'VE dropped in to whisper some secrets I've heard,
  Between you and me and the Post!
Picked up on the wing by a 'cute little bird.
We are gentlemen 'ere — so the caution's absurd,
Still, you'll please to remember that every word
  Is between you and me and the Post!

Chorus (to which the singer should dance).

Between you and me and the Post! An 'int is
    sufficient at most.
I'd very much rather this didn't go farther, than
    'tween you and me and the Post!

At Lord Sorlsbury's table there's sech a to-do.
  Between you and me and the Post!
When he first ketches sight of his dinner *menoo*,
And sees he's set down to good old Irish stoo —
Which he's sick of by this time — now, tell me,
    ain't *you?*
  Between you and me and the Post!

(This happy and pointed allusion to the Irish Question is sure to provoke loud laughter from an audience of Radical sympathies. For Unionists,

the words "Lord Sorlsbury's" *can be altered by our patent reversible method into* "the G. O. M.'s," *without at all impairing the satire.)*   *Chorus, as before.*

The G. O. M.'s hiding a card up his sleeve.
  Between you and me and the Post!
Any ground he has lost he is going to retrieve,
And what *his* little game is, he'll let us perceive,
And he'll pip the whole lot of 'em, so I believe,
  Between you and me and the Post!
       (*Chorus.*)

(*The hit will be made quite as palpably for the other side by substituting* "Lord Sorlsbury's," *etc., at the beginning of the first line, should the majority of the audience be found to hold Conservative views.*)

Little Randolph won't long be left out in the cold.
  Between you and me and the Post!
If they let him inside the Conservative fold,
He has promised no longer he'll swagger and
  scold,
But to be a good boy, and to do as he's told,
  Between you and me and the Post!
       (*Chorus.*)

(*The mere mention of* Lord Randolph's *name is sufficient to ensure the success of any song.*)

Joey Chamberlain's orchid's a bit overblown,
    Between you and me and the Post!

(*This is rather subtle, perhaps, but an M. H.
audience will see a joke in it somewhere, and
laugh.*)

'Ow to square a round table I'm sure he has shown.
            (*Same observation applies here.*)

But of late he's been leaving his old friends alone,
And I fancy he's grinding an axe of his own,
    Between you and me and the Post!
            (*Chorus.*)

(*We now pass on to Topics of the Day, which we
treat in a light but trenchant fashion.*)

On the noo County Councils they've too many nobs,
    Between you and me and the Post!
For the swells stick together, and sneer at the
    mobs;
And it's always the rich man the poor one who
    robs.
We shall 'ave the old business — all jabber and
    jobs!
    Between you and me and the Post!
            (*Chorus.*)

(N. B. *This verse should not be read to the* L. C. C.,
who might miss the fun of it.)

There's a new rule for ladies presented at Court,
  Between you and me and the Post!
High necks are allowed, so no colds will be
  cort,
But I went to the droring-room lately, and
  thort
Some old wimmen had dressed quite as low as
  they *ort!*
  Between you and me and the Post!
     (*Chorus.*)

By fussy alarmists we're too much annoyed,
  Between you and me and the Post!
If we don't want our neighbors to think we're
  afroid,
    [*M. H. rhyme.*
Spending dibs on defence we had better avoid,
And give 'em instead to the poor unemployed.
    [*M. H. political economy.*
  Between you and me and the Post! ·
     (*Chorus.*)

This style of perlitical singing ain't hard,
  Between you and me and the Post!
As a " Mammoth Comique " on the bills I am ·
  starred,

And, so long as I'm called, and angcored, and
    hurrar'd,
I can rattle off rubbish like this by the yard,
    Between you and me and the Post!

[*Chorus, and dance off to sing the same song — with
or without alterations — in another place.*

III.—A DEMOCRATIC DITTY.

THE following example, although it gives a not wholly inadequate expression to what are understood to be the loftier aspirations of the most advanced and earnest section of the New Democracy, should not be attempted, as *yet*, before a West-End audience. In South or East London, the sentiment and philosophy of the song may possibly excite rapturous enthusiasm; in the West-End, though the tone is daily improving, they are not educated quite up to so exalted a level at present. Still, as an experiment in proselytism, it might be worth risking, even there. The title it bears is:—

GIVEN AWAY—WITH A POUND OF TEA!

VERSE I.—(*Introductory.*)

SOME Grocers have taken to keeping a stock
Of ornaments — such as a vase, or a clock —
With a ticket on each, where the words you may
    see :—
" To be given away — with a Pound of Tea!"

Chorus (in waltz time)..

" Given away ! "

That's what they say.

Gratis — a present it's offered you free.

Given away,

With nothing to pay,

" Given away — [*tenderly*] — with a Pound of Tea ! "

VERSE II. — (*Containing the moral reflection.*)

Now, the sight of those tickets gave me an idear.

What it set me a-thinking you're going to 'ear :

I thought there were things that would possibly be

Better given away — with a Pound of Tea !

Chorus. — " Given away." So much as to say, etc.

VERSE III. — (*This, as being rather personal than general in its application, may need some apology. It is really put in as a graceful concession to the taste of an average Music-hall audience, who like to be assured that the artists who amuse them are as unfortunate as they are erratic in their domestic relations.*)

Now, there's my old Missus who sits up at 'ome —

And when I sneak *up*-stairs my 'air she will comb, —

I don't think I'd call it bad business if *she*
Could be given away — with a Pound of Tea!

Chorus. — " Given away ! "   That's what they say,
    etc.   [*Mutatis mutandis.*

VERSE IV. — (*Flying at higher game.   The social
satire here is perhaps almost too good-natured,
seeing what intolerable pests all peers are to the
truly Democratic mind.   But we must walk before
we can run.   Good-humored contempt will do
very well, for the present.*)

Fair Americans snap up the pick of our Lords.
It's a practice a sensible Briton applords.

[*This will check any groaning at the mention of
Aristocrats.*

Far from grudging our Dooks to the pretty
    Yan-kee, —
(*Magnanimously.*)   Why, we'd give 'em away —
    with a Pound of Tea!

Chorus. — Give 'em away!   So we all say, etc.

VERSE V. — (*More frankly Democratic still.*)
To-wards a Republic we're getting on fast;
Many old institootions are things of the past.

(*Philosophically.*) Soon the Crown 'll go, too, as
>   an a-nomalee,

And be given away — with a Pound of Tea!

Chorus. — "Given away!" Some future day, etc.

VERSE VI. — (*Which expresses the peaceful procliv-
ities of the populace with equal eloquence and
wisdom. A welcome contrast to the era when
Britons had a bellicose and immoral belief in the
possibility of being called upon to defend themselves at some time!*)

We've made up our minds — though the Jingoes
>   may jor —

Under no provocation to drift into war!

So the best thing to do with our costly Na-vee

Is — Give each ship away, with a Pound of Tea!

>   *Chorus.* — Give 'em away, etc.

VERSE VII. — *We cannot well avoid some refer-
ence to the Irish Question in a Music-hall ditty,
but observe the logical and statesmanlike method
of treating it here. The argument — if crudely
stated — is borrowed from some advanced by our
foremost politicians.*)

We've also discovered at last that it's crule

To deny the poor Irish their right to 'Ome Rule!

So to give 'em a Parlyment let us agree —
(*Rationally.*)   Or they may blow us up with a
    Pound of their " Tea " !

[*A euphemism which may possibly be remembered
  and understood.*

      Chorus. — Give it away, etc.

VERSE VIII. (*culminating in a glorious prophetic
    burst of the Coming Dawn.*)

Iniquitous burdens and rates we'll relax :
For each "h" that's pronounced we will clap on a
    tax !
            [*A very popular measure.*
And a nouse in Belgraveyer, with furniture free,
Shall each Soshalist sit in, a-taking his tea!

Chorus, and dance off. — Given away ! Ippipooray !
    Gratis we'll get it for nothing and free !
Given away !   Not a penny to pay !   Given away !
    — with a Pound of Tea !

If this Democratic Dream does not appeal
favorably to the imagination of the humblest
citizen, the popular tone must have been misrepresented by many who claim to act as its chosen
interpreters — a supposition *Mr. Punch* must decline to entertain for a single moment.

IV. — THE IDYLLIC.

THE following ballad will not be found above the heads of an average audience, while it is constructed to suit the capacities of almost any lady *artiste.*

SO SHY!

The singer should, if possible, be of mature age, and inclined to a comfortable embonpoint. As soon as the bell has given the signal for the orchestra to attack the prelude, she will step upon the stage with that air of being hung on wires, which seems to come from a consciousness of being a favorite of the public.

I'M a dynety little dysy of the dingle,

[*Self-praise is a great recommendation — in Music-hall songs.*

So retiring and so timid and so coy.
If you ask me why so long I have lived single,
 I will tell you — 'tis because I am so shoy.

[*Note the manner in which the rhyme is adapted to meet Arcadian peculiarities of pronunciation.*

39

Spoken. — Yes, I am — really, though you wouldn't think it to look at me, would you? But, for all that, —

Chorus.

When I'm spoken to, I wriggle,
Going off into a giggle,
And as red as any peony I blush ;
   Then turn paler than a lily,
   For I'm such a little silly,
That I'm always in a flutter or a flush!

[*After each chorus an elaborate step dance, expressive of shrinking maidenly modesty.*

I've a cottage far away from other houses,
   Which the nybours hardly ever come anoigh ;
When they do, I run and hoide among the rouses,
   For I *cannot* cure myself of being shoy.

Spoken. — A great girl like me, too ! But there, it's no use trying, for —

Chorus. — When I'm spoken to, I wriggle, etc.

Well, the other day I felt my fice was crimson,
   Though I stood and fixed my gyze upon the
      skoy,
For at the gyte was sorcy Chorley Simpson,
   And the sight of him's enough to turn me shoy.

Spoken. — It's singular, but Chorley always 'as that effect on me.

Chorus. — When he speaks to me, I wriggle, etc.

Then said Chorley: "My pursuit there's no
    evyding.
Now I've caught you, I insist on a reploy.
Do you love me?   Tell me truly, little myding!"
    But how *is* a girl to answer when she's shoy?

Spoken. — For even if the conversation happens to be about nothing particular, it's just the same to me.

Chorus. — When I'm spoken to, I wriggle, etc.

There we stood among the loilac and syringas,
    More sweet than any Ess. Bouquet you boy;
                      [*Arcadian for* "*buy.*"
And Chorley kept on squeezing of my fingers,
    And I couldn't tell him not to, being shoy.

Spoken. — For, as I told you before, —

Chorus. — When I'm spoken to, I wriggle, etc.

Soon my slender wyste he ventured on embrycing,
    While I only heaved a gentle little soy;
Though a scream I would have liked to rise my
    vice in,
    It's so difficult to scream when you are shoy!

Spoken. — People have such different ways of
listening to proposals. As for me, —

Chorus. — When they talk of love, I wriggle, etc.

So very soon to Church we shall be gowing.
  While the bells ring out a merry peal of jy.
If obedience you do not hear me vowing.
  It will only be because I am so shy.

  [*We have brought the rhyme off legitimately at last,
  it will be observed.*

Spoken. — Yes, and when I'm passing down the
oil. on Chorley's arm. with everybody looking at
me. —

Chorus.

  I am certain I shall wriggle.
  And go off into a giggle.
And as red as any peony I'll blush.
  Going through the marriage service
  Will be sure to mike me nervous.
          [*Note the freedom of the rhyme.*
And to put me in a flutter and a flush !

V. — THE AMATORY EPISODIC.

THE history of a singer's latest love — whether fortunate or otherwise — will always command the interest and attention of a Music-hall audience. Our example, which is founded upon the very best precedents, derives an additional piquancy from the social position of the beloved object. Cultivated readers are requested not to shudder at the rhymes. *Mr. Punch's* Poet does them deliberately and in cold blood, being convinced that without these somewhat daring concords no ditty would have the slightest chance of satisfying the great ear of the Music-hall public.

The title of the song is : —

MASHED BY A MARCHIONESS.

The singer should come on correctly and tastefully attired in a suit of loud dittoes, a startling tie, and a white hat — the orthodox costume (on the Music-hall stage) of a middle class swain suffering from love-sickness. The air should be of the conventional jog-trot and jingle order, chastened by a sentimental melancholy.

I'VE lately gone and lost my 'art — and where
    you'll never guess —
I'm regularly mashed upon a lovely Marchioness !

'Twas at a Fancy Fair we met, inside the Albert
    'All ;
So affable she smiled at me as I came near her
    stall !

Chorus.

Don't tell me Belgravia is stiff in behavior !
    She'd an Uncle an Earl, and a Dook for her Pa —
    Still there was no starchiness in that fair Mar-
      chioness,
    As she stood at her stall in the Fancy Bazaar !

At titles and distinctions once I'd ignorantly scoff,
As if no bond could be betwixt the tradesman and
    the toff !
I held with those who'd do away with difference
    in ranks —
But that was all before I met the Marchioness of
    Manx !

    Chorus. — Don't tell me Belgravia, etc.

A home was being started by some kind aristo-cràts,
For orphan kittens, born of poor, but well-con-
    nected cats ;
And of the swells who planned a *Fête* this object
    to assist,
The Marchioness of Manx's name stood foremost
    on the list.

    Chorus. — Don't tell me Belgravia, etc.

I never saw a smarter hand at serving in a shop,

For every likely customer she caught upon the 'op!

And from the form her ladyship displayed at that
Bazaar,

(*With enthusiasm*) — You might have took your
oath she'd been brought up behind a bar!

Chorus. — Don't tell me Belgravia, etc.

In vain I tried to kid her that my purse had been
forgot,

She spotted me in 'alf a jiff, and chaffed me
precious hot!

A sov. for one regaliar she gammoned me to spend.

" You really can't refuse," she said, " I've bitten
off the end! "

Chorus. — Don't tell me Belgravia, etc.

" Do buy my crewel-work," she urged, " it goes
across a chair,

You'll find it come in useful, as I see you 'ile your
'air! "

So I 'anded over thirty bob, though not a coiny
bloke.

I couldn't tell a Marchioness how nearly I was
broke!

Spoken. — Though I *did* take the liberty of say-
ing, "Make it fifteen bob, my lady!" But she
said, with such a fascinating look — I can see it
yet! — "Oh, I'm sure *you*'re not a 'aggling kind
of a man," she says, "you haven't the face for it.
And think of all them pore fatherless kittings,"
she says ; " think what thirty bob means to *them !* "
says she, glancing up so pitiful and tender under
her long eyelashes at me. Ah, the Radicals may
talk as they *like*, but —

       Chorus. — Don't tell me Belgravia, etc.

A raffle was the next concern I put my rhino in :
The prize a talking parrot, which I didn't want to
     win.
Then her sister, Lady Tabby, showed a painted
     milking-stool,
And I bought it — though it's not a thing I sit on
     as a rule.

Spoken. — Not but what it was a handsome article
in its way, too, — had a snow-scene with a sunset
done in oil on it. "It will look lovely in your
chambers," says the Marchioness ; " it was ever so
much admired at Catterwall Castle ! " It didn't
look so bad in my three-pair back, I must say,

though unfortunately the sunset came off on me
the very first time I happened to set down on it.
Still, think of the condescension of painting such
a thing at all !

Chorus. — Don't tell me Belgravia, etc.

The Marquis kept a-fidgeting and frowning at his
    wife,
For she talked to me as free as if she'd known me
    all my life !
I felt that I was in the swim, so wasn't over-
    awed,
But 'ung about and spent my cash as lavish as a
    lord !

Spoken. — It was worth all the money, I can tell
you, to be chatting there across the counter with a
real live Marchioness for as long as ever my funds
would 'old out. They'd have held out much
longer, only the Marchioness made it a rule never
to give change — she couldn't break it she
said, not even for *me*. I wish I could give you
an idea of how she smiled as she made that
remark; for the fact is, when an aristocrat *does*
unbend — well, —

Chorus. — Don't tell me Belgravia, etc.

Next time I meet the Marchioness a-riding in the
    Row,
I'll ketch her eye and raise my 'at, and up to her
    I'll go,
(*With sentiment*) — And tell her next my 'art I
    keep the stump of that cigar
She sold me on the 'appy day we 'ad at her Bazaar!

Spoken. — And she'll be pleased to see me again,
I know! She's not one of your stuck-up sort;
don't you make no mistake about it, the aristoc-
racy ain't 'alf as bloated as people imagine who
don't *know* 'em. Whenever I hear parties running
'em down, I always say, —

Chorus.

Don't tell me Belgravia is stiff in behavior, etc.

VI. — THE CHIVALROUS.

The singer (who should be a large man, in evening dress, with a crumpled shirt-front) will come on the stage with a bearing intended to convey at first sight that he is a devoted admirer of the fair sex. After removing his crush-hat in an easy manner, and winking airily at the orchestra, he will begin : —

WHY SHOULDN'T THE DARLINGS?

THERE'S enthusiasm brimming in the breasts of
    all the women,
And they're calling for enfranchisement with
    clamor eloquent:
When some parties in a huff rage at the plea for
    Female Suffrage,
I invariably floor them with a simple argu-ment.

Chorus (to be rendered with a winning persuasive-ness).

Why *shouldn't* the darlings have votes ? de-ar
    things !
On politics each of 'em dotes, de-ar things !

(*Pathetically.*)   Oh it it *does* seem so hard
    They should all be debarred,
'Cause they happen to wear petticoats, de-ar
    things!

Nature all the hens to crow meant, I could prove
    it in a moment,
   Though they've selfishly been silenced by the
    cockadoodledoos.
But no man of sense afraid is of enfranchising the
    Ladies.
   (*Magnanimously.*)   Let 'em put their pretty
    fingers into any pie they choose!
Spoken. — For —
    Chorus. — Why *shouldn't* the darlings, etc.

They would cease to care for dresses, if we made
    them electresses,
   No more time they'd spend on needlework, nor
    at pianos strum ;
Every dainty little Dorcas would be sitting on a
    Caucus,
   Busy wire-pulling to produce the New Millen-
    ni-um!
Spoken. — Oh! —
    Chorus. — Why *shouldn't* the darlings, etc.

In the House we'll see them sitting soon, it will be
only fitting,
They should have an opportunity their country's laws to frame.
And the Ladies' legislation will be sure to cause
sensation,
For they'll do away with everything that seems
to them a shame !

Spoken. — Then —

Chorus. — Why *shouldn't* the darlings, etc.

They will promptly clap a stopper on whate'er
they deem improper,
Put an end to vaccination, landed property, and
· pubs ;
And they'll fine Tom, Dick, and Harry, if they
don't look sharp and marry,
And for Kindergartens confiscate those nasty
horrid Clubs !

Spoken. — Ah ! —

Chorus. — Why *shouldn't* the darlings, etc.

They'll declare it's quite immoral to engage in
foreign quarrel,
And that Britons never, never will be warriors
any more !

When our forces are abolished, and defences all
    demolished,
They will turn upon the Jingo tack, and want
    to go to war!

Spoken. — So —

    . *Chorus.* — Why *shouldn't* the darlings, etc.

(*With a grieved air.*) Yet there's some who'd close
    such vistars to their poor . down-trodden
    sistars,
And persuade 'em, if they're offered votes,
    politely to refuse!
Say they do not care about 'em, and would rather
    be without 'em —
Oh, I haven't common patience with such narrer-
    minded views!

Spoken. — No! —

    Chorus. — Why *shouldn't* the darlings, etc.

And it's females — that's the puzzle! — who peti-
    tion for the muzzle,
Which I call it poor and paltry, and I think
    you'll say so too.

They are not in any danger. Let 'em drop the
    dog-in-manger!
If they don't require the vote themselves, there's
    other Ladies do!

Spoken. — And —

    Chorus. — Why *shouldn't* the darlings, etc.

[*Here the singer will gradually retreat backwards to
the rear of the stage, open his crush-hat, and ex-
tend it in an attitude of triumph as the curtain
descends.*

VII. — THE FRANKLY CANAILLE.

ANY ditty which accurately reflects the habits and amusements of the people is a valuable human document — a fact that probably accounts for the welcome which songs in the following style invariably receive from Music-hall audiences generally. If — MR. PUNCH presumes — they conceived such pictures of their manner of spending a holiday to be unjustly or incorrectly drawn in any way, they would protest strongly against being so grossly misrepresented. As they do nothing of the sort, no apology can be needed for the following effusion, which several ladies now adorning the Music-hall stage could be trusted to render with immense effect. The singer should be young and charming, and attired as simply as possible. Simplicity of attire imparts additional piquancy to the words : —

THE POOR OLD 'ORSE.

WE 'ad a little outing larst Sunday arternoon ;
And sech a jolly lark it was, I sha'n't forget it
    soon !

We borrered an excursion van to take us down to
    Kew,
And — oh, we did enjoy ourselves! I don't mind
    telling *you.*

[*This to the Chef d'Orchestre, who will assume a*
    polite interest.

[*Here a little spoken interlude is customary.* Mr. P.
    does not venture to do more than indicate this by a
    synopsis, the details can be filled in according to
    the taste and fancy of the fair artiste: — " *Yes,*
    we did 'ave a time, I can assure yer." The party:
    " *Me and* Jimmy 'Opkins; " *old* " Pa Plapper."
    Asked because he lent the van. The meanness
    of his subsequent conduct. " Aunt Snapper; "
    her imposing appearance in her " cawfy-colored
    front." Bill Blazer; *his* " *girl," and his accord-*
    ion. Mrs. Addick (*of the fried fish emporium*
    around the corner) ; *her gentility —* " *Never seen*
    out of her mittens, and always the lady, no matter
    how much she may have taken." From this work
    round by an easy transition to —

The Chorus.

For we 'ad to stop 'o course,
Jest to bait the bloomin' 'orse,

So we'd pots of ale and porter
(Or a drop o' something shorter),
While he drunk his pail o' water,
He was sech a whale on water!
That more water than he oughter,
More water than he oughter,
   'Ad the old 'orse!

Second Stanza.

That 'orse he was a rum 'un — a queer old quad-
  ru-pèd,
At every public-'ouse he passed he'd cock his art-
  ful 'ed!
Sez I, " If he goes on like this, we sha'n't see
  Kew to-night!"
Jim 'Opkins winks his eye, and sez, " We'll git
  along all right!"

 Chorus. — Though we 'ave to stop o' course, etc.
   [*With slight textual modifications.*

Third Stanza.

At Kinsington we 'alted, 'Ammersmith, and Turn-
  ham Green,
The 'orse 'ad sech a thust on him, its like was
  never seen!

With every 'arf a mile or so, that animal got
    blown :
And we was far too well brought-up to let 'im
    drink alone !

      Chorus. — As we 'ad to stop, o' course, etc.

        Fourth Stanza.

We stopped again at Chiswick, till at last we got
    to Kew,
But when we reached the Gardings — well, there
    was a fine to-do !
The Keeper, in his gold-laced tile, was shutting-to
    the gate,
Sez he, " There's no admittance now — you're just
    arrived too late ! "

[*Synopsis of spoken interlude : Spirited passage-at-
arms between* Mr. Wm. Blazer *and the* Keeper;
singular action of Pa Plapper ; " *I want to see yer
Pagoder — bring out yer old Pagoder as you're so
proud on !* " Mrs. Addick's *disappointment at
not being able to see the* " *Intemperate Plants*,"
and the " *Pitcher Shrub*," *once more. Her subsi-
dence in tears, on the floor of the van.* Keeper
*concludes the dialogue by inquiring why the party
did not arrive sooner.* An' we sez, " Well, it was
like this, ole cock robin — d'yer see ? "

      Chorus. — We've 'ad to stop, o' course, etc.

Fifth Stanza.

"Don't fret," I sez, "about it, for they ain't got
much to see

Inside their precious Gardings — so let's go and
'ave some tea!

A cup I seem to fancy now — I feel that faint and
limp —

With a slice of bread-and-butter, and some creases,
and a s'rimp!"

[*Description of the tea:* — "*And the s'rimps — well,
I don't want to say anything against the s'rimps
— but it* did *strike me they were feelin' the 'eat a
little — s'rimps are liable to it, and you can't prevent 'em." After tea. The only tune* Mr. Blazer
*could play on his accordion. Tragic end of that
instrument. How the party had a "little more
lush." Scandalous behavior of "*Bill Blazer's
*girl." The company consume what will be ele-
gantly referred to as "a bit o' booze."* Aunt
Snapper "*gets the 'ump." The outrage to her
front. The proposal to start — whereupon, "*Mrs.
Addick, *who was a'-settin' on the geraniums in the
winder, smilin' at her boots, which she'd just took
off because she said they stopped her breathing,"
protested that there was no hurry, considering that —
Chorus, as before.* — We've got to stop, o' course, etc.

Sixth Stanza.

But when the van was ordered, we found — what
    do yer think?

[*To the* Chef d'Orchestre, *who will affect complete
ignorance.*

That miserable 'orse 'ad been an' took too much to
    drink!
He kep' a-reeling round us, like a circus worked
    by steam,
And, 'stead o' keeping singular, he'd turned into a
    team!

[*Disgust of the party :* Pa Plapper *proposes to go
back to the inn for more refreshment, urging —*

Chorus.

    We must wait awhile o' course,
    Till they've sobered down the 'orse.
    Just another pot o' porter,
    Or a drop o' something shorter,
    While our good landlady's daughter
    Takes him out some soda-warter.
    For he's 'ad more than he oughter,
    He's 'ad more than he oughter,
            'As the poor old 'orse!

Seventh Stanza.

So, when they brought the 'orse round, we started
    on our way :
'Twas 'orful 'ow the animal from side to side would
    sway !
Young 'Opkins took the reins, but soon in slumber
    he was sunk —

(*Indignantly.*)   When a interfering Copper ran us
    in for being drunk !

[*Attitude of various members of the party. Un-
warrantable proceeding on the part of the* Constable. *Remonstrance by* Pa Plapper *and the
company generally in* —

Chorus.

Why, can't yer shee ? o' coursh
Tishn't us — it ish the 'orsh !
He's a whale at swilling water,
We've 'ad only ale and porter,
Or a drop o' something shorter,
You le'mme go, you shnorter !
Don' you tush me till you oughter !
Jus' look 'ere — to cut it shorter —
      Take the poor old 'orsh !

[*General adjournment to the Police-station. Interview with the* Magistrate *on the following morning.*
Mr. Hopkins *called upon to state his defence,
replies in* —

Chorus.

Why, your wushup sees, o' course,
It was all the bloomin' 'orse!
He *would* 'ave a pail 'o water
Every 'arf a mile (or quarter),
Which is what he didn't oughter!
He shall stick to ale or porter,
With a drop o' something shorter,
I'm my family's supporter —
          Fine the poor old 'orse!

[*The* Magistrate's *view of the case. Concluding remark that, notwithstanding the success of the excursion, as a whole — it will be some time before
the singer consents to go upon any excursion with
a horse of such bibulous tendencies as those of the
quadruped they drove to* Kew.

VIII.—THE DRAMATIC SCENA.

THIS is always a popular form of entertainment, demanding, as it does, even more dramatic than vocal ability on the part of the artist. A song of this kind is nothing if not severely moral, and frequently depicts the downward career of an incipient drunkard with all the lurid logic of a Temperance Tract. *Mr. Punch*, however, is inclined to think that the lesson would be even more appreciated and taken to heart by the audience, if a slightly different line were adopted, such as he has endeavored to indicate in the following example : —

THE DANGER OF MIXED DRINKS.

The singer should have a great command of facial expression, which he will find greatly facilitated by employing (as indeed is the usual custom) colored limelight at the wings.

First Verse (to be sung under pure white light).

HE (*these awful examples are usually, and quite properly, anonymous*) was once as nice a fellow as you could desire to meet,

Partial to a pint of porter, always took his spirits
  neat ;

Long ago a careful mother's cautions trained her
  son to shrink

From the meretricious sparkle of an aërated drink.

Refrain (showing the virtuous youth resisting temp-
tation. N. B. The refrain is intended to be
spoken through music. Not sung).

> Here's a pub that's handy.
>   Liquor up with you?
> Thimbleful of brandy?
>   Don't mind if I do.
> Soda-water? No, sir.
>   Never touch the stuff.
> Promised mother — so, sir.
>   (*With an upward glance.*)
>   'Tisn't good enough !

Second Verse. (*Primrose light for this.*)

Ah, how little we suspected, as we saw him in his
  bloom,

What a demon dogged his footsteps, luring to an
  awful doom !

Vain his mother's fond monitions ; soon a friend,
  with fiendish laugh,

Tempts him to a quiet tea-garden, plies him there
  with shandy-gaff !

Refrain (illustrating the first false step).

> Why, it's just the mixture
>> I so long have sought!
> Here I'll be a fixture
>> Till I've drunk the quart!
> Just the stuff to suit yer.
>> Waiter, do you hear?
> Make it, for the future,
>> *Three* parts ginger-beer!

Third Verse (requiring violet-tinted slide).

By-and-by, the ale discarding, ginger-beer he craves alone.

Undiluted he procures it, buys it bottled up in stone.

(*The earthenware bottles are said by connoisseurs to contain liquor of superior strength and quality.*)

From his lips the foam he brushes — crimson overspreads his brow.

To his brain the ginger's mounting! Could his mother see him now!

Refrain (depicting the horrors of a solitary debauch poisoned by remorse).

> Shall I have another?
> Only ginger-pop!

(*Wildly.*)   Ah! I promised mother
   Not to touch a drop!
Far too much I'm tempted.
   (*Recklessly.*)   Let me drink my fill!
That's the fifth I've emptied —
   Oh, I feel so ill!
[*Here the singer will stagger about the boards.*

Fourth Verse.   (*Turn on lurid crimson ray for this.*)

Next with drinks they style " teetotal " he his
   manhood must degrade ;
Swilling effervescent sirups — " ice-cream soda,"
   " raspberryade,"
Koumiss tempts his jaded palate — payment he's
   obliged to bilk —
Then, reduced to destitution, finds forgetfulness
   in — milk !

Refrain (*indicating rapid moral deterioration*).
   What's that on the railings?
      [*Point dramatically at imaginary area.*
   Milk — and in a can !
   Though I have my failings,
      I'm an honest man.
         [*Spark of expiring rectitude here.*

I cannot resist it.

        [Pantomime of opening can.

That celestial blue!

Has the milkman missed it?

        [Melodramatically.

I'll be missing too!

Fifth Verse (in pale blue light).

Milk begets a taste for water, so comparatively cheap,

Every casual pump supplies him, gratis, with potations deep;

He at every drinking-fountain pounces on the pewter cup,

Conscious of becoming bloated, powerless to give it up!

Refrain (illustrative of utter loss of self-respect).

" Find one straight before me? "

    Bobby, you're a trump!

Faintness stealing o'er me —

    Ha — at last — a pump!

If that little maid 'll

    Just make room for one,

I could grab the ladle

    After she has done.

*The last verse is the culminating point of this moral
drama: The miserable wretch has reached the
last stage. He shuts himself up in his cheerless
abode, and there, in shameful secrecy, consumes
the element for which he is powerless to pay — the
inevitable Nemesis following.*

*Sixth Verse (all lights down in front. Ghastly
green light at wings).*

Up his sordid stairs in secret to the cistern now he
    steals,
Where, amidst organic matter, gambol microscopic
    eels;
Tremblingly he turns the tap on — not a trickle
    greets the trough!
For the stony-hearted turncock's gone and cut his
    water off!

*Refrain (in which the profligate is supposed to de-
mand an explanation from the turncock, with a
terrible dénoûment).*

    " Rate a quarter owing,
        Comp'ny stopped supply."
    " Set the stream a-flowing,
        Demon — or you die!"
    " Mercy! — ah! you've choked me!"
    [*In hoarse, strangled voice as the turncock.*

" *Will* you turn the plug ? "

> [*Savagely as the hero.*

"No !   [*Faintly, as turncock.*

[*Business of flinging a corpse on stage, and regard-
ing it terror-stricken.   A long pause : then, in a
whisper,* —

> " The fool provoked me !

(*With a maniac laugh.*)   Horror !   I'm a Thug ! "

[*Here the artist will die, mad, in frightful agony, and
rise to bow his acknowledgments.*

IX.—THE DUETTISTS.

The " Duet and Dance " form so important a feature in Music-hall entertainments, that they could hardly, with any propriety, be neglected in a model compilation such as *Mr. Punch's*, and it is possible that he may offer more than one example of this blameless diversion. For some reason or other, the habit of singing in pairs would seem to induce a pessimistic tone of mind in most Music-hall *artistes*, and — why, *Mr. Punch* does not pretend to say — this cynicism is always more marked when the performers are of the softer sex. Our present study is intended to fulfil the requirements of the most confirmed female sceptic, and, though the Message of the Music Halls may have been given worthier and fuller expression by pens more practised in such compositions, *Mr. Punch* is still modestly confident that this ditty, with all its shortcomings, can be sung in any Music Hall in the Metropolis without exciting any sentiment other than entire approval of the teaching it conveys. One drawback, indeed, it has, but that concerns the performers alone. For the sake of affording contrast and relief, it was thought ex-

pedient that one of the fair duettists should profess an optimism which may — perhaps must —
tend to impair her popularity. A conscientious
artiste may legitimately object, for the sake of her
professional reputation, to present herself in so
humiliating a character as that of an *ingénue*, and
a female "Juggins;" and it does seem as if the
Cynical Sister must inevitably monopolize the
sympathies of an enlightened audience. However, this difficulty is less formidable than it appears; it should be easy for the Unsophisticated
Sister to convey a subtle suggestion here and
there, possibly in the incidental dance between the
verses, that she is not really inferior to her
partner in smartness and knowledge of the world.
But perhaps it would be the fairest arrangement
if the Sisters could agree to alternate so ungrate-
ful a *rôle*.

RHINO!

First Verse.

FIRST SISTER (*placing three of the fingers of her
left hand on her heart, and extending her right
arm in timid appeal*).

DEAR sister, of late I'm beginning to doubt
If the world is as black as they paint it.
It mayn't be as bad as some try to make out —

SECOND SISTER (*with an elaborate mock courtesy*).
That *is* a discovery! *Mayn't* it?
FIRST S. (*abashed*). I'm sure there are sev'ral
who aren't a bad lot.
And some sort of principle seem to have got,
For they act on the square—
SECOND S. Don't you talk tommy-rot!
It's done for advertisement, *ain't* it?

Refrain.

SECOND S. Why, there's nobody at bottom any
better than the rest!
FIRST S. Are you sure of it?
SECOND S. I'm telling you, and *I* know,
The principle they act upon's whatever pays 'em
best.
And the only real religion now is—Rhino!
[*The last word must be rendered with full metallic
effect. A step-dance, expressive of conviction on
one part, and incipient wavering on the other,
should be performed between the verses.*

Second Verse.

FIRST S. (*returning, shaken, to the charge*). Some
*un*married men lead respectable lives.
SECOND S. (*decisively*). Well, *I've* never happened to meet them!

First S.   There are husbands who're always polite to their wives.

Second S.   Of course — if their better halves beat them!

First S.   Some tradesmen have consciences, so I've heard said;

Their provisions are never adulterated,

But they treat all their customers fairly instead.

Second S.   'Cause they don't find it answer to cheat them!

Refrain.

First S.   { What?
Second S. { No, — They're none of 'em at bottom any better than the rest.

Second S.   I'm speaking from experience, and *I* know.

If you could put a window-pane in everybody's breast

You'd see on all the hearts was written — "Rhino!"

Third Verse.

First S.   There are girls you can't tempt with a title or gold.

Second S.   There may be — but I've never seen one.

First S. Some much prefer love in a cottage,
I'm told.

Second S. (*putting her arms a-kimbo*). If you
swallow *that*, you're a green one!

They'll stick to their lover so long as he's cash,

When it's gone, they look out for a wealthier
mash.

A girl on the gush talks unpractical trash —

When it comes to the point, she's a keen one!

Refrain.

First S. Then are none of us at bottom any
better than the rest?

Second S. (*cheerfully*). Not a bit; I am a girl
myself, and *I* know.

First S. You'd surely never give your hand to
some one you detest?

Second S. Why *rather* — if he's rolling in the
Rhino!

Fourth Verse.

First S. Philanthropists give up their lives to
the poor.

Second S. It's chiefly with tracts they present
them.

First S. Still, some self-denial I'm sure they
endure?

SECOND S.   It's their hobby, and seems to content them.

FIRST S.   But don't they go into those horrible slums?

SECOND S.   Sometimes — with a flourish of trumpets and drums.

FIRST S.   I've heard they've collected magnificent sums.

SECOND S.   And nobody knows how they've spent them!

Refrain.

SECOND S.   Oh, they're none of 'em at bottom any better than the rest!

They are only bigger hypocrites, as *I* know;

They've famous opportunities for feathering their nest,

When so many fools are ready with the Rhino!

Fifth Verse.

FIRST S.   Our Statesmen are prompted by duty alone.

SECOND S. (*compassionately*).   Whoever's been gammoning *you* so?

FIRST S.   They wouldn't seek office for ends of their own?

SECOND S.   What else would induce 'em to do so?

First S.   But Time, Health, and Money they all
    sacrifice.

Second S.   I'd do it myself at a quarter the price.

There's pickings for all, and they needn't ask
    twice,

    For they're able to put on the screw so!

Refrain (together).

No, they're none of 'em at bottom any better than
    the rest!

    They may kid to their constituents — but *I*
    know;

Whatever lofty sentiments their speeches may
    suggest,

    They regulate their actions by the Rhino!

[*Here the pair will perform a final step-dance, in-
dicative of enlightened scepticism, and skip off in
an effusion of sisterly sympathy, amidst enthu-
siastic applause.*

X. — DISINTERESTED PASSION.

WHEN a Music-hall singer does not treat of the tender passion in a rakish and knowing spirit, he is apt to exhibit an unworldliness truly ideal in its noble indifference to all social distinctions. So amiable a tendency deserves encouragement, and *Mr. Punch* has much pleasure in offering the following little idyl to the notice of any Mammoth Comique who may happen to be in a sentimental mood. It is supposed to be sung by a scion of the nobility, and the *artiste* will accordingly present himself in a brown "billy-cock" hat, a long gray frock-coat, fawn-colored trousers, white "spats," and primrose, or green gloves — the recognized attire of a Music-hall aristocrat. A powerful — though not necessarily tuneful — voice is desirable for the adequate rendering of this ditty: any words it is inconvenient to sing, can always be spoken.

ONLY A LITTLE PLEBEIAN!

First Verse.

WHEN first I met my Mary Ann, she stood behind
    a barrow —
  A bower of enchantment spread with many a
    dainty snack!
And, as I gazed, I felt my heart transfixed with
    Cupid's arrow,
  For she opened all her oysters with so. fairylike
    a knack.

Refrain (throaty, but tender).

She's only a little Plebeian!
  And I'm a Patrician swell!
But she's as sweet as Aurora, and how I adore her,
  No eloquence ever can tell!
Only a fried-fish vend-ar!
  Selling her saucers of whilks,

    [*Almost defiant stress on the word "whilks."*

But, for me, she's as slend-ar — far more true and
    tend-ar,
  Than if she wore satins and silks!

[*The grammar of the last two lines is shaky, but the
  Lion-Comique must try to put up with that, and,*

after all, does sincere emotion ever stop to think
about grammar ?   If it does, Music-hall audiences
don't — which is the main point.

Second Verse.

I longed before her little feet to grovel in the
    gutter :
  I vowed, unless I won her as a wife, 'twould
    drive me mad !
Until at last a shy consent I coaxed her lips to
    utter,
For she dallied with her Anglo-Dutch, and whis-
    pered, " Speak to Dad ! "

  Refrain. — For she's only a little Plebeian, etc.

Third Verse.

I called upon her sire, and found him lowly born,
    but brawny,
  A noble type, when sober, of the British artisan ;
I grasped his honest hand, and didn't mind its
    being horny :
" Behold ! " I cried, " a suitor for your daughter,
    Mary Ann ! "

Refrain. — Though she's only a little Plebeian, etc.

Fourth Verse.

" You ask me, gov'nor, to resign," said he, " my
only treasure,
And so a toff her fickle heart away from me has
won ! "
He turned to mask his manly woe behind a pewter
measure —
Then, breathing blessings through the beer, he
said, " All right, my son !

Refrain. — If she's only a little Plebeian,
And you're a Patrician swell," etc.

Fifth Verse.

(*The author flatters himself that, in quiet sentiment
and homely pathos he has seldom done anything
finer than the two succeeding stanzas.*)

Next I sought my noble father in his old ancestral
castle,
And at his gouty foot my love's fond offering
I laid —
A simple gift of shellfish, in a neat brown-paper
parcel!
" Ah, Sir ! " I cried, " If you could know, you'd
love my little maid ! "

Refrain. — True, she's only a little Plebeian, etc.

Sixth Verse.

Beneath his shaggy eyebrows soon I saw a tear-
  drop twinkle ;
  That artless present overcame his stubborn Nor-
    man pride !
And when I made him taste a whilk, and try a
  periwinkle,
  His last objection vanished — so she's soon to be
    my bride !
Refrain. — Ah ! she's only a little Plebeian, etc.

Seventh Verse.

Now heraldry's a science that I haven't studied
  much in,
  But I mean to ask the College — if it's not
    against their rules —
That three periwinkles proper may be quartered
  on our 'scutcheon,
With a whilk regardant, rampant, on an oyster-
  knife, all gules !
Refrain. — As she's only a little Plebeian, etc.

This little ditty, which has the true unmistak-
able ring about it, and will, *Mr. Punch* believes,
touch the hearts of any Music-hall audience, is
entirely at the service of any talented *artiste* who
will undertake to fit it with an appropriate melody,
and sing it in a spirit of becoming seriousness.

XI. — THE PANEGYRIC PATTER.

THIS ditty is designed to give some expression to the passionate enthusiasm for nature which is occasionally observable in the Music-hall song-stress. The young lady who sings these verses will of course appear in appropriate costume; viz., a large white hat and feathers, a crimson sunshade, a pink frock, high-heeled sand-shoes, and a liberal extent of black silk stockings. A phonetic spelling has been adopted where necessary to bring out the rhyme, for the convenience of the reader only, as the singer will instinctively give the vowel-sounds the pronunciation intended by the author.

THE JOYS OF THE SEA-SIDE.

First Verse.

OH, I love to sit a-gyzing on the boundless blue horizing,

  When the scorching sun is blyzing down on sands, and ships, and sea!

And to watch the busy figgers of the happy little
    diggers,
  Or to listen to the niggers when they choose to
     come to me !

Chorus (to which the singer should sway in waltz-
            time).

    For I'm offully fond of the *Sea*-side !
    If I'd only my w'y, I would *de*-cide
        To dwell evermore,
        By the murmuring shore,
    With the billows a-blustering *be*-side !

Second Verse.

Then how pleasant of a morning, to be up before
    the dorning !
And to sally forth a-prorning — e'en if nothing
    back you bring !
Some young men who like fatigue 'll go and try
    to pot a sea-gull,
  What's the odds if it's illegal, or the bird they
     only wing ?

Chorus. — For it's one of the sports of the *Sea*-
    side ! etc.

Third Verse.

Then what j'y to go a bything — though you'll
swim, if you're a sly thing,
    Like a mermaid nimbly writhing, with a foot
upon the sand!
When you're tired of old Poseidon, there's the
pier to promenide on,
    Strauss, and Sullivan, and Haydn form the pro-
gramme of the band.

Chorus.— For there's always a band at the *Sea-*
side! etc.

Fourth Verse.

And, with boatmen so beguiling, sev'ral parties go
out siling!
    Sitting all together smiling, handing sandwiches
about,
To the sound of concertiner, — till they're gradually greener,
And they wish the ham was leaner, as they sip
their bottled stout.

Chorus. — And they cry, "Put us back on the *Sea-*
side!" etc.

Fifth Verse.

There is pleasure unalloyed in hiring hacks and
     going roiding!
  (If you stick on tight, avoiding any cropper or
     mishap.)
Or about the rocks you ramble; over bowlders slip
     and scramble;
  Or sit down and do a gamble, playing " Loo " or
     " Penny Nap."

Chorus. — " Penny Nap " is the gyme for the *Sea-
     side!* etc.

Sixth Verse.

Then it's lovely to be spewning, all the glamour of
     the mewn in,
With your love his banjo tewning, ere flirtation
     can begin!
As along the sands you're strowling, till the hour
     of ten is towling,
  And your ma, severely scowling, asks " Wher-
     ever you have bin!"

Chorus. — Then you answer " I've been by the *Sea-
     side!* " etc.

Seventh Verse.

Should the sky be dark and frowning, and the
restless winds be mowning.
　With the breakers' thunder drowning all the
　laughter and the glee;
And the day should prove a drencher, out of doors
you will not ventcher,
　But you'll read the volumes lent yer by the
　Local Libraree!

Chorus. — For there's sure to be one at the *Sea-*
side! etc.

Eighth Verse.

If the weather gets no calmer, you can patronize
the dramer,
　Where the leading lady charmer is a chit of
　forty-four!
And a duty none would shirk is to attend the
strolling circus,
　For they'd all be in the workhouse, should their
　antics cease to dror!

Chorus. — And they're part of the joys of the *Sea-*
side! etc.

Encore Verse (to be used only in case of emergency).

Well, I reelly must be gowing — I've just time to
    make my bow in —
  But I thank you for allowing me to patter on so
    long.
And if, like me, you're pining for the breezes
    there's some brine in,
  Why, I'll trouble you to jine in with the chorus
    to my song!

Chorus (all together). — Oh, we're offully fond of
    the *Sea*-side ! etc.

XII.—THE PLAINTIVELY PATHETIC.

A MUSIC-HALL audience will always be exceedingly susceptible to pathos — so long as they clearly understand that the song is not intended to be of a comic nature. However, there is very little danger of any misapprehension in the case of our present example, which is as natural and affecting a little song as any that have been moving the Music-Halls of late. The ultra-fastidious may possibly be repelled by what they would term the vulgarity of the title, — " The Night-light Ever Burning by the Bed " — but, although it is true that this humble luminary is now more generally called a " Fairy Lamp," persons of true taste and refinement will prefer the homely simplicity of its earlier name. The song only contains three verses, which is the regulation allowance for Music-hall pathos, the authors probably feeling that the audience could not stand any more. It should be explained that the " tum-tum " at the end of certain lines is not intended to be sung — it is merely an indication to the orchestra to pinch their violins in a *pizzicato* manner. The singer should either come on as a serious black man, — for burnt cork is a marvellous provocative of pathos, — or as his ordinary self. In either case he should wear evening dress, with a large brilliant on each hand.

THE NIGHT-LIGHT EVER BURNING BY THE BED.

First Verse.

I'VE been thinking of the home where my early
>   years were spent,
>   'Neath the care of a kind maiden aunt (*Tum-tum-tum!*),
And to go there once again has been often my
>   intent,
>   But the railway fare's expensive, so I can't!
>   (*Tum-*tum!)
Still I never can forget that night when last we
>   met:
>   "Oh, promise me — whate'er you do!" she
>   said (*Tum-tum-tum!*),
"Wear flannel next your chest, and when you go
>   to rest,
>   Keep a night-light always burning by your
>   bed!" (*Tum-*tum!)

Refrain (pianissimo).

And my eyes are dim and wet;

For I seem to hear them yet —

Those solemn words at parting that she said

(*Tum*-tum-*tum!*):

"Now, mind you burn a night-light,

— 'Twill last until it's quite light —

In a saucerful of water by your bed!"

(*Tum*-tum!)

Second Verse.

I promised as she wished, and her tears I gently
dried,

As she gave me all the half-pence that she had.
(*Tum*-tum-*tum!*)

And through the world e'er since I have wandered
far and wide,

And been gradually going to the bad! (*Tum*-
tum!)

Many a folly, many a crime I've committed in my
time,

For a lawless and a checkered life I've led!
(*Tum*-tum-*tum!*)

Still I've kept the promise sworn — flannel next
my skin I've worn,

And I've always burnt a night-light by my bed!
(*Tum*-tum!)

Refrain.

All unhallowed my pursuits,
(Oft to bed I've been in boots!)
Still o'er my uneasy slumber has been shed (*Tum-*
tum-*tum!*)
The moderately bright light
Afforded by a night-light,
In a saucerful of water by my bed!   (*Tum*-tum!)

Third Verse. (*To be sung with increasing solemnity.*)

A little while ago, in a dream my aunt I saw;
In her frill-surrounded night-cap there she
stood!   (*Tum*-tum-*tum!*)
And I sought to hide my head 'neath the counter-
pane in awe,
And I trembled — for my conscience isn't good!
(*Tum*-tum!)
But her countenance was mild — so indulgently
she smiled
That I knew there was no further need for
dread!   (*Tum*-tum-*tum!*)
She had seen the flannel vest enveloping my chest,
And the night-light in its saucer by my bed!
(*Tum*-tum!)

Refrain (more pianissimo still).

But ere a word she spoke,
I unhappily awoke!
And away, alas! the beauteous vision fled! (*Tum-tum-tum!*)
(*In mournful recitation*). — There was nothing but
the slight light
Of the melancholy night-light
That was burning in a saucer by my bed!
(*Tum*-tum!)

XIII. — THE MILITARY IMPER-
SONATOR.

To be a successful Military Impersonator, the
principal requisite is a uniform, which may be
purchased for a moderate sum, second-hand, in
the neighborhood of almost any barracks. Some
slight acquaintance with the sword exercise and
elementary drill is useful, though not absolutely
essential. Furnished- with these, together with a
few commanding attitudes, and a song possessing
a spirited, martial refrain, the Military Impersonator may be certain of an instant and striking
success upon the Music-hall stage, — especially if
he will condescend to avail himself of the ballad
provided by *Mr. Punch*, as a vehicle for his
peculiar talent. And, though we say it ourselves, it is a very nice ballad, to which Mr.
McDougall himself would find it difficult to take
exception. It is in three verses, too, — the limit
understood to be formally approved by the London
County Council for such productions. It may be,
indeed, that (save so far as the last verse illus-
trates the heroism of our troops in action — a

heroism too real and too splendid to be rendered ridiculous, even by Military Impersonators), the song does *not* convey a particularly accurate notion of the manner and pursuits of an officer in the Guards. But then no Music-hall ditty can ever be accepted as a quite infallible authority upon any social type it may undertake to depict — with the single exception, perhaps, of the Common (or Howling) Cad. So that any lack of actuality here will be rather a merit than a blemish in the eyes of an indulgent audience. Having said so much, we will proceed to our ballad, which is called, —

IN THE GUARDS!

First Verse.

I'M a Guardsman, and my manner is perhaps a bit
     " haw-haw ; "
But when you're in the Guards you've got to show
     esprit de corps.
              [*Pronounce " a spreedy core."*
We look such heavy swells, you see, we're all
     aristo-cràts,
When on parade we stand arrayed in our 'eavy
     bearskin 'ats.

Chorus (during which the Martial Star will march round the stage in military order).

We're all "'Ughies," "Berties," "Archies,"
    In the Guards! Doncher know?
Twisting silky long mustarches,
        [*Suit the action to the word here.*
Bein' Guards! Doncher know?
While our band is playing Marches,
    For the Guards! Doncher know?
And the ladies stop to gaze upon the Guards,
        Bing-*Bang!*

[*Here a member of the orchestra will oblige with the cymbals, while the vocalist performs a military salute, as he passes to —*

Second Verse.

With duchesses I'm 'and in glove, with countesses
    I'm thick;
From all the nobs I get invites — they say I am
    "so *chic!*"
        [*Pronounce "chick."*
It often makes me laugh to read, whene'er I go off
    guard,
"Dear Bertie, come to my At Home!" on a coronetted card!

Chorus.

For we're " Berties," " 'Ughies," " Archies,"
      In the Guards! Doncher know?
With our silky long mustarches,
      In the Guards! Doncher know?
Where's a regiment that marches
      Like the Guards? Doncher know?
All the darlings — bless 'em! — dote upon the
    Guards,
               Bing-*Bang!*

Third Verse.

[*Here comes the singer's great chance, and, by merely
taking a little pains, he may make a tremendously
effective thing out of it. If he can manage to
slip away between the verses, and change his bear-
skin and scarlet coat for a solar topee and kharkee
tunic at the wings, it will produce an enormous
amount of enthusiasm, only he must not take* more
*than five minutes over this alteration, or the
audience — so curiously are British audiences con-
stituted — may grow impatient for his return.*

But hark! the trumpet sounds! . . . (*Here a
member of the orchestra will oblige upon the trumpet.*) What's this? . . . (*The singer will take a
folded paper from his breast and peruse it with
attention.*) We're ordered to the front!

[*This should be shouted.*

We'll show the foe how " Carpet-Knights " can
face the battle's brunt!

They laugh at us as " Brummels " — but we'll
prove ourselves " Bay-yards!"

[*Now the Martial Star will draw his sword and un-
fasten his revolver-case, taking up the exact pose
in which he is represented upon the posters outside.*

As you were! . . . Form Square! . . . Mark
Time! . . . Slope Arms! . . . now —'Tention!
. . . (*These military evolutions should all be
gone through by the artist.*)   Forward, Guards!

[*To be yelled through music.*

Chorus.

Onward every 'ero marches,
          In the Guards! Doncher know?
All the " 'Ughies," " Berties," " Archies,"
          Of the Guards! Doncher know?
They may twist their long mustarches,
          For they're Guards! Doncher know?
Dandies? yes, — but dandy *lions* are the Guards!
                    Bing-*Bang!*

[*Red fire and smoke at wings, as curtain falls upon
the Military Impersonator in the act of changing
to a new attitude.*

MODEL MUSIC HALL.

DRAMAS.

I. — THE LITTLE CROSSING-SWEEPER.

DRAMATIS PERSONÆ.

THE LITTLE CROSSING-SWEEPER. ⎱ . . MISS JENNY JIKNS.
By the unrivalled Variety Artist ⎰

THE DUKE OF DILLWATER . . . MR. HENRY IRVING.

[*Specially engaged; Mr. Punch is sure that he will cheerfully make some slight sacrifice for so good a cause, and he can easily slip out and get back again between the Acts of Henry the Eighth.*"

A POLICEMAN . . . . MR. RUTLAND BARRINGTON

[*Engaged, at enormous expense, during the entire run of this piece.*

A BUTLER (*his original part*) . . . . MR. ARTHUR CECIL.

FOOT-PASSENGERS, FLUNKEYS, BURGLARS. — By the celebrated Knockabout Quick-change Troupe.

SCENE I. —*Exterior of the* DUKE'S *mansion in Euston Square by night. On the right, a realistic moon (by kind permission of* PROFESSOR HERKOMER) *is rising slowly behind a lamp-post. On left centre, a practicable pillar-box, and crossing, with real mud. Slow music, as* MISS JENNY JINKS *enters, in rags, with broom. Various characters cross the street, post letters, etc.;* MISS JINKS *follows them, begging piteously for a cop-*

per, which is invariably refused, whereupon she assails them with choice specimens of street sarcasm — which the lady may be safely trusted to improvise for herself.

MISS JENNY JINKS (*leaning despondently against pillar-box, on which a ray of limelight falls in the opposite direction to the moon*).

Ah, this cruel London, so marble-'arted and vast,
Where all who try to act honest are condemned to
    fast!

    Enter two BURGLARS *cautiously.*

FIRST B. (*to* MISS J. J.)   We can put you up to a
    fake as will be worth your while,
For you seem a sharp, 'andy lad, and just our
    style!

[*They proceed to unfold a scheme to break into the Ducal abode, and offer* MISS J. *a share of the spoil, if she will allow herself to be put through the pantry window.*

MISS J. J. (*proudly*).   I tell yer I won't 'ave
    nothink to do with it, fur I ain't been used
To sneak into the house of a Dook to whom I
    'aven't been introdooced!

SECOND BURGLAR (*coarsely*).   Stow that snivel,
    yer young himp, we don't want none of
    that bosh!

MISS J. J. (*with spirit*).   You hold *your* jaw —
    for, when you opens yer mouth, there ain't
    much o' yer face left to wash!

[*The* BURGLARS *retire, baffled, and muttering.*
    MISS J. *leans against pillar-box again — but*
    more irresolutely.

I've arf a mind to run after 'em, I 'ave, and tell
    'em I'm game to stand in! . . .

But ah, — didn't my poor mother say as Burglary
    was a *Sin!*

[DUKE *crosses stage in a hurry; as he pulls out*
    his latchkey, a threepenny bit falls unregarded,
    except by the little SWEEPER, *who pounces*
    eagerly upon it.

What's this?   A bit o' good luck at last for a
    starvin' orfin boy!

What shall I buy?   *I* know — I'll have a cup of
    cawfy, and a prime saveloy!

Ah, — *but it ain't mine* — and 'ark . . . that music
    up in the air!
                    [*A harp is heard in the flies.*

Can it be mother a-playin' on the 'arp to warn her
    boy to beware?

(*Awestruck.*) There's a angel voice that is sayin'
plain (*solemnly*), " Him as prigs what isn't
his'n ;

Is sure to be copped some day — and then — his
time he will do in prison ! "

[*Goes resolutely to the door, and knocks. The*
Duke *throws open the portals.*

Miss J. J. If yer please, sir, was you aware as
you've dropped a thruppenny-bit?

The Duke (*after examining the coin*). 'Tis the
very piece I have searched for everywhere !
You rascal, you've *stolen it!*

Miss J. J. (*bitterly*). And *that's* how a Dook
rewards honesty in *this* world !

[*This line is sure of a round of applause.*

The Duke (*calling off*). Policeman, I give this
lad in charge for a shameless attempt to
rob,

Enter Policeman.

Unless he confesses instantly who put him up to
the job !

Miss J. J. (*earnestly*). I've told yer the bloomin'
truth, I 'ave — or send I may die !

I'm on'y a Crossing-sweeper, sir, but I'd scorn to
tell yer a lie !

Give me a quarter of an hour — no more — just
time to kneel down and pray,

As I used to at mother's knee long ago — then
the Copper kin lead me away.

[*Kneels in limelight. The* POLICEMAN *turns
away, and uses his handkerchief violently; the*
DUKE *rubs his eyes.*

THE DUKE. No, blow me if I can do it, for I
feel my eyes are all twitching!

(*With conviction.*) If he's good enough to kneel
by his mother's side, he's good enough to be
in my kitching!

[DUKE *dismisses* CONSTABLE, *and, after disap-
pearing into the mansion for a moment, returns
with a neat page's livery, which he presents to
the little* CROSSING-SWEEPER.

MISS J. J. (*naïvely*). 'Ow much shall I ask for
on this, Sir? What! Yer don't mean to
say they're for *me!*

Am I really to be a Page to one of England's
proud aristocra-cee?" [*Does some steps.*

Mechanical change to SCENE II. — *State apartment
at the* DUKE'S. *Magnificent furniture, gilding,
chandeliers. Suits of genuine old armor. Statuary (lent by British and Kensington Museums).*

Enter MISS J., *with her face washed, and looking particularly plump in her page's livery. She wanders about stage, making any humorous comments that may occur to her on the armor and statuary. She might also play tricks on the butler, and kiss the maids — all of which will serve to relieve the piece by delicate touches of comedy, and delight a discriminating audience.*

Enter the DUKE.

I hope, my lad, that we are making you comfortable here?   [*Kindly.*

MISS J. J.   Never was in such slap-up quarters in my life, sir, *I'll* stick to yer, no fear!

[*In the course of conversation the* DUKE *learns, with aristocratic surprise, that the* PAGE'S *mother was a singer at the Music Halls.*

MISS J. J.   What, don't know what a Music-'all's like? and you a Dook! Well, you *are* a jolly old juggins! 'Ere, you sit down on this gilded cheer — that's the ticket — I'll bring you your champagne and your cigars — want a light? (*Strikes match on her pantaloons.*) Now you're all comfortable.

The DUKE *sits down, smiling indulgently, out of her way, while she introduces her popular Vocal Character Sketch, of which space only permits us to give a few specimen verses.*

First the Champion Comic
 Steps upon the stage;
With his latest " Grand Success,"
 Sure to be the rage!
Sixty pounds a week he
 Easily can earn;
Round the Music Halls he goes,
 And does at each a " turn."

Illustration.

Undah the stors in a sweet shady dairl,
I strolled with me awm round a deah little gairl,
And whethaw I kissed har yaw'd like me to tairl —
 Well, I'd rawthah you didn't inquiah!

All golden her hair is,
 She's queen of the Fairies,
And known by the name of the lovely Mariah,
 She's a regular Venus,
 But what passed between us,
I'd very much rawthah you didn't inquiah!

> Next the Lady Serio,
>   Mincing as she walks ;
> If a note's too high for her,
>   She doesn't sing — she talks,
> What she thinks about the men
>   You're pretty sure to learn,
> She always has a hit at them,
>   Before she's done her " turn !"

Illustration.

You notty young men, ow! you notty young men!
You tell us you're toffs, and the real Upper Ten,
But behind all your ears is the mark of a pen!
So don't you deceive us, you notty young men!

Miss J. J. (*concluding*).   And such, sir, are these
        entertainments grand,
In which Mirth and Refinement go 'and-in-'and!

[*As the* Duke *is expressing his appreciation of the
elevating effect of such performances, the* Butler
rushes in, followed by two flurried Footmen.

Butler.   Pardon this interruption, my Lord, but
        I come to announce the fact
That by armed house-breakers the pantry has just
        been attacked!

DUKE.   Then we'll repel them — each to his
  weapons look!
I know how to defend my property, although I
  am a Dook!
MISS J. J. (*snatching sword from one of the men-
  in-armor*).
With such a weapon I their hash will settle!
You'll lend it, won't yer, old Britannia Metal?
[*Shouts and firing without; the* FOOTMEN *hide
  under sofa.*
Let flunkeys flee — though danger may encircle us,
A British Buttons ain't afeard of Burgulars!
[*Tremendous firing, during which the* BURGLARS
  are supposed to be repulsed with heavy loss by the
  DUKE, BUTLER, *and* PAGE.
MISS J. J.   'Ere — I say, Dook, I saved yer life,
  didn't yer *know?*
(*A parting shot, upon which she staggers back with
  a ringing scream.*)
The Brutes! they've been and shot me! . . .
  Mother . . . Oh!
[*Dies in limelight and great agony; the* FOOTMEN
  *come out from under sofa and regard with sorrow-
  ing admiration the lifeless form of the* LITTLE
  CROSSING-SWEEPER, *which the* DUKE, *as curtain
  falls, covers reverently with the best table-cloth.*

II.—JOE, THE JAM-EATER.

A MUSICAL SPECTACULAR AND SENSATIONAL INTERLUDE.

(Dedicated respectfully to Mr. McDougall and the L. C. C.)

THE Music-hall Dramatist, like Shakspeare and Molière, has a right to take his material from any source that may seem good to him. *Mr. Punch*, therefore, makes no secret of the fact that he has based the following piece upon the well-known poem of "The Purloiner," by the Sisters Jane and Ann Taylor, who were *not*, as might be too hastily concluded, "Song and Dance Duettists," but two estimable ladies, who composed "cautionary" verses for the young, and whose works are a perfect mine of wealth for Moral Dramatists. In this dramatic version the author has tried to infuse something of the old Greek sense of an overruling destiny, without detriment to prevailing ideas of moral responsibility. Those who have the misfortune to be born with a propensity for illicit jam, may learn from our drama the terrible results of failing to overcome it early in life.

JOE, THE JAM-EATER.

Dramatis Personæ.

Jam-Loving Joe. By that renowned Melodramatic Serio-Comic, Miss Connie Curdler.

Joe's Mother (*the very part for Mrs. Bancroft, if she can only be induced to make her reappearance*).

John, a Gardener. By the great Pink-eyed Unmusical Zulu.

Jim-Jam, the Fermentation Fiend. By Mr. Beerbohm Tree (*who has kindly consented to undertake the part*).

Chorus of Plum and Pear Gatherers *from the Savoy* (*by kind permission of Mr. D'Oyly Carte*).

Scene. — *The Store-room at sunset, with view of exterior of Jam Cupboard, and orchard in distance.*

Enter Joe.

"As Joe was at play, Near the cupboard one day, When he thought no one saw but himself." — *Vide Poem.*

Joe (*dreamily*). 'Tis passing strange that I so
  partial am
To playing in the neighborhood of Jam!

[*Here* MISS CURDLER *will introduce her great humorous Satirical Medley illustrative of the Sports of Childhood, and entitled,* "Some little Gymes we all of us 'ave Plied;" *after which, enter* JOE'S *mother, followed by* JOHN *and the Chorus, with baskets, ladders, etc., for gathering fruit.*

"His Mother and John, To the garden had gone, To gather ripe pears and ripe plums." — *Poem.*

JOE'S MOTHER (*with forced cheerfulness*) —

Let's hope, my friends, to find our pears and
    plums,

Unharmed by wopses, and untouched by wums.

[*Chorus signify assent in the usual manner, by holding up the right hand.*

Solo. — JOHN.

Fruit, when gathered ripe is wholesome —
    Otherwise if eaten green.

Once I knew a boy who stole some —

[*With a glance at* JOE, *who turns aside to conceal his confusion.*

His internal pangs were keen!

CHORUS (*virtuously*).   'Tis the doom of all who're
    mean,

Their internal pangs are keen!

JOE'S MOTHER (*aside*). By what misgivings is a
mother tortured!

I'll keep my eye on Joseph in the orchard.

[*She invites him with a gesture to follow.*

JOE (*earnestly*). Nay, Mother, here I'll stay till
you have done.

Temptation it is ever best to shun!

JOE'S MOTHER. So laudable his wish, I would
not cross it—

(*Mysteriously.*) He knows not there are jam-pots
in yon closet!

Chorus.

Away we go tripping,
From boughs to be stripping
Each pear, plum, and pippin
    Pomona supplies!
When homeward we've brought 'em,
Those products of autumn,
We'll carefully sort 'em
    (*One of our old Music-hall rhymes*).
According to size!

[*Repeat as they caper out.*

[JOE'S MOTHER, *after one fond, lingering look behind, follows: the voices are heard more and more
faintly in the distance. Stage darkens: the last
ray of sunset illumines key of jam-cupboard door.*

JOE.   At last I am alone! Suppose I tried
That cupboard — just to see what's kept inside?

[*Seems drawn towards it by some fatal fascination.*

There *might* be Guava jelly, and a plummy cake,
For such a prize I'd laugh to scorn a stomach-ache!

[*Laughs a stomach-ache to scorn.*

And yet (*hesitating*), who knows ? — a pill . . .
    perchance — a powder!
(*Desperately.*) What then? To scorn I'll laugh
    them — even louder!

[*Fetches chair and unlocks cupboard. Doors fall
    open with loud clang, revealing interior of jam-
    closet (painted by* HAWES CRAVEN). JOE
    mounts chair to explore shelves.*

" How sorry I am, He ate raspberry jam, And currants that
    stood on the shelf ! " — *Vide Poem.*

JOE (*speaking with mouth full and back to audience*).
'Tis raspberry — of all the jams my favorite ;
I'll clear the pot, whate'er I have to pay for it !
And finish up with currants from this shelf. . . .
Who'll ever see me?

The DEMON *of the jam-closet* (*rising slowly from an
    immense pot of preserves*). No one — but My-
    self !

[*The cupboard is lit by an infernal glare (cour-
teously lent by the Lyceum Management from
"Faust" properties); weird music.* JOE *turns
slowly, and confronts the* DEMON *with awestruck
eyes.* N.B. — *Great opportunity for powerful
acting here.*

THE DEMON (*with a bland sneer*). Pray don't
    mind *me* — I will await your leisure.

JOE (*automatically*). Of your acquaintance, sir,
    I've not the pleasure.

Who are you? Wherefore have you intervened?

THE DEMON (*quietly*). My name is "Jim-Jam;"
    occupation — fiend.

JOE (*cowering limply on his chair*). O Mr. Fiend,
    I *know* it's very wrong of me!

DEMON (*politely*). Don't mention it — but please
    to come "along of" me?

JOE (*imploringly*). Do let me off this once, —
    ha! you're relenting,

You smile —

DEMON (*grimly*). 'Tis nothing but my jam fer-
    menting!

[*Catches* JOE'S *ankle, and assists him to descend.*

JOE. You'll drive me mad!

DEMON (*carelessly*). I *may* — before I've done
    with you!

JOE.   What do you want?

DEMON (*darkly*).   To have a little fun with you!
Of fiendish humor now I'll give a specimen.

[*Chases him round and round stage, and proceeds
to smear him hideously with jam.*

JOE (*piteously*).   Oh, don't! I feel *so* sticky.
      What a mess I'm in!

DEMON (*with affected sympathy*).   That *is* the
      worst of jam — it's apt to stain you.

[*To* JOE, *as he frantically endeavors to remove the
traces of crime.*

I see you're busy — so I'll not detain you!

[*Vanishes down stair-trap with a diabolical laugh.
Cupboard-doors close with a clang; all lights
down.* JOE *stands gazing blankly for some
moments, and then drags himself off stage. His*
MOTHER *and* JOHN, *with pear and plum gatherers bearing laden baskets, appear at doors at
back of scene, in faint light of torches.*

Re-enter JOE, *bearing a candle and wringing his
hands.*

JOE.   Out, jammed spot!   What — will these
      hands *never* be clean?
Here's the smell of the raspberry jam still!   All

the powders of Gregory cannot unsweeten this little hand. . . . (*Moaning.*) Oh, oh, oh!

[*This passage has been accused of bearing too close a resemblance to one in a popular stage play; if so, the coincidence is purely accidental, as the dramatist is not in the habit of reading such profane literature.*

JOE'S MOTHER. Ah! what an icy dread my heart benumbs!

See — stains on all his fingers, *and* his thumbs!

"What Joe was about, His mother found out, When she look'd at his fingers and thumbs." —*Poem again.*

Nay, Joseph — 'tis your mother . . . speak to her!

JOE (*tonelessly, as before*). Lady, I know you not (*touches lower part of waistcoat*); but, prithee, undo this button. I think I have jam in all my veins, and I would fain sleep. When I am gone, lay me in a plain white jelly-pot, with a parchment cover, and on the label write — but come nearer, I have a secret for your ear alone . . . there are strange things in *some* cupboards! Demons should keep in the dust-bin. (*With a ghastly smile.*) I know not what ails me, but I am not feeling at all well.

[*Joe's Mother stands a few steps from him, with her hands twisted in her hair, and stares at him in speechless terror.*

Joe (*to the Chorus*).   I would shake hands with you all, were not my fingers so sticky.   We eat marmalade, but we know not what it is made of. Hush! if Jim-Jam comes again, tell him that I am not at home.   Loo-loo-loo!

All (*with conviction*).   Some shock has turned his brine!

Joe (*sitting down on floor, and weaving straws in his hair*).   My curse upon him that invented jam. Let us all play Tibbits.

[*Laughs vacantly; all gather round him, shaking their heads, his Mother falls fainting at his feet as curtain falls upon a strong and moral, though undeniably gloomy dénoûment.*

III.—THE MAN-TRAP.

THIS drama, which, like our last, has been suggested by a poem of the Misses Taylor, will be found most striking and impressive in representation upon the Music-hall stage. The dramatist has ventured to depart somewhat from the letter, though not the spirit, of the original text, in his desire to enforce the moral to the fullest possible extent. Our present piece is intended to teach the great lesson that an inevitable Nemesis attends apple-stealing in this world, and that Doom cannot be disarmed by the intercession of the evil-doer's friends, however well-meaning.

THE MAN-TRAP.

A THRILLING MORAL MUSICAL SENSATION SKETCH IN ONE SCENE.

DRAMATIS PERSONÆ.

WILLIAM (*a Good Boy*) . . MR. HARRY NICHOLLS.

THOMAS (*a Bad Boy*) . . MR. HERBERT CAMPBELL.
(*Who have kindly offered their services.*)

BENJAMIN (*neither one thing nor the other*), MR. SAMUEL SUPER.

THE MONSTER MAN-TRAP . MR. GEORGE CONQUEST.

SCENE. — *An elaborate set, representing, on extreme left, a portion of the highroad, and wall dividing it from an orchard; realistic apple and pear trees laden with fruit. Time, about four o'clock on a hot afternoon. Enter* WILLIAM *and* THOMAS, *hand-in-hand, along road; they ignore the dividing wall, and advance to front of stage.*

Duet. — WILLIAM *and* THOMAS.

WM.   I'm a reg'lar model boy, I am; so please make no mistake.

It's Thomas who's the bad 'un — *I'm* the good!

THOS.   Yes, I delight in naughtiness, for naughtiness's sake,

And I wouldn't be like William if I could!

Chorus.

WM.   Ever since I could toddle, my conduct's been model,

There's, oh, such a difference between me and him!

THOS.   While still in the cradle, I orders obeyed ill,

And now I've grown into a awful young limb!

TOGETHER.   Yes, now $\left\{ \begin{array}{l} \text{he's} \\ \text{I've} \end{array} \right\}$ grown into a awful young limb.

I've made up my mind not to imitate *him!*

[*Here they dance.*

Second Verse.

WM. If some one hits him in the eye, he always
hits them back !

When *I* am struck, my Ma I merely tell !

On passing fat pigs in a lane, he'll give 'em each a
a whack !

THOS. (*impenitently*). And jolly fun it is to
hear 'em yell ! [*Chorus.*

Third Verse.

WM. He's always cribbing coppers — which he
spends on lollipops.

THOS. (A share of which *you*'ve never yet
refused !)

WM. A stone he'll shy at frogs and toads, and
anything that hops !

THOS. (While you look on, and seem to be
amused !) [*Chorus.*

Fourth Verse.

WM. As soon as school is over, Thomas goes
a-hunting squirr'ls,

Or butterflies he'll capture in his hat !

THOS. *You* play at Kissing in the Ring with all
the little girls !

WM. (*demurely*). Well, Thomas, I can see no harm
in *that !* [*Chorus.*

Fifth Verse.

WM. Ah, Thomas, if you don't reform, you'll
come to some bad end!

THOS. Oh, William, put your head inside a bag!

WM. No, Thomas, that I cannot — till you promise to amend!

THOS. Why, William, what a chap you are to nag!

[*Chorus and dance.* THOMAS *returns to road, and
regards the apple-trees longingly over top of wall.*

THOS. Hi, William, look ... what apples! there
— don't *you* see?

And pears — my eye! just *ain't* they looking juicy!

WM. Nay, Thomas, since you're bent upon a sin,

I will walk on, and visit Benjamin!

[*Exit* WILLIAM (L. 2 E.), *while* THOMAS *proceeds
to scale the wall and climb the boughs of the nearest pear-tree. Melodramatic Music. The* MON-
STER MAN-TRAP *stealthily emerges from long grass
below, and fixes a baleful eye on the unconscious*
THOMAS.

THOS. I'll fill my pockets, and on pears I'll feast!
[*Sees* MAN-TRAP, *and staggers.*

Oh, lor — whatever is that hugly beast!

Hi, help, here! call him off! . . .

THE MONSTER.   'Tis vain to holler —
My horders are — all trespassers to swoller!
You just come down — I'm waiting 'ere to ketch
    you.
(*Indignantly.*) You *don't* expect I'm coming up to
    fetch you!
THOS. (*politely*). Oh, not if it would inconvenience
    you, sir!
(*In agonized aside.*) I feel my grip grow every
    moment looser!

The MONSTER, *in a slow, uncouth manner, proceeds
to scramble up the tree.*

Oh, here's a go! The horrid thing can *climb!*
Too late I do repent me of my crime!

[*Terrific sensation chase! The* MONSTER MAN-
TRAP *leaps from bough to bough with horrible
agility, and eventually secures his prey, and leaps
with it to the ground.*

THOS. (*in the* MONSTER'S *jaws*). I'm sure you
    seem a kind, good-natured creature —
You will not harm me?
MONSTER.   No — I'll only eat yer!

[THOMAS *slowly vanishes down its cavernous jaws;
faint yells are heard at intervals — then nothing*

but a dull champing sound; after which, dead silence. The MONSTER *smiles, with an air of repletion.*

Re-enter WILLIAM, *from* R., *with* BENJAMIN.

BENJAMIN.   I'm very glad you came — but where
  is Thomas?

WM. (*severely*).   Tom is a wicked boy, and better
  from us,

For on the road he stopped to scale a wall! . . .

> [*Sees* MAN-TRAP, *and starts.*

What's *that?*

BENJ.   It will not hurt *good* boys at all —
It's only Father's Man-trap — why so pale?

WM.   The self-same tree! . . . the wall that Tom
  would scale!

Where's Thomas *now?*   Ah, Tom, the wilful pride
  of you!

[*The* MAN-TRAP *affects an elaborate unconsciousness.*

BENJ. (*with sudden enlightenment*).   Man-trap, I do
  believe poor Tom's inside of you!

That sort of smile's exceedingly suspicious.

> [*The* MAN-TRAP *endeavors to hide in the grass.*

WM.   Ah, Monster, give him back — 'tis true he's
  vicious,

And had no business to go making free with you!
But think, so bad a boy will disagree with you!

[WILLIAM *and* BENJAMIN *kneel in attitudes of entreaty on either side of the* MAN-TRAP, *which shows signs of increasing emotion as the song proceeds.*

BENJAMIN (*sings*).

Man-trap, bitter our distress is,
    That you have unkindly penned
In your innermost recesses
    One who used to be our friend!

WILLIAM (*sings*).

In his downward course arrest him!
    (He may take a virtuous tack);
Pause awhile, ere you digest him,
    Make an effort — bring him back!

The MAN-TRAP *is convulsed by a violent heave;* WILLIAM *and* BENJAMIN *bend forward in an agony of expectation, until a small shoe and the leg of* THOMAS'S *pantaloons are finally emitted from the* MONSTER'S *jaws.*

BENJ. (*exultantly*). See, William, now he's coming . . . here's his shoe for you!

THE MAN-TRAP (*with an accent of genuine regret*).
    I'm sorry — but that's all that I can do for you!

WM. (*raising the shoe and the leg of pantaloons, and
    holding them sorrowfully at arm's length*).
    He's met the fate which moralists all prom-
    ise is

The end of such depraved careers as Thomas's!

Oh, Benjamin, take warning by it *be*-time!

(*More brightly*).   But now to wash our hands —
    'tis nearly tea-time!

[*Exeunt* WILLIAM *and* BENJAMIN, *to wash their
    hands, as* Curtain *falls.* N. B. — *This finale is
    more truly artistic, and in accordance with modern
    dramatic ideas, than the conventional "picture."*

IV.—THE FATAL PIN.

Our present example is pure tragedy of the most ambitious kind, and is, perhaps, a little in advance of the taste of a Music-hall audience of the present day. When the fusion between the Theatres and the Music Halls is complete — when Miss Bessie Bellwood sings "*What Cheer, Ria?*" at the Lyceum, and Mr. Henry Irving gives his compressed version of *Hamlet* at the Trocadero; when there is a general levelling-up of culture, and removal of prejudice — then, and not till then, will this powerful little play meet with the appreciation which is its due. The main idea is suggested by the Misses Taylor's well-known poem, *The Pin*, though the dramatist has gone further than the poetess in working out the notion of Nemesis.

THE FATAL PIN.

A TRAGEDY.

Dramatis Personæ.

Emily Heedless. By either Miss Vesta Tilley or Mrs. Bernard Beere.

Peter Paragon. Mr. Forbes Robertson or Mr. Arthur Roberts (only he mustn't sing "*The Good Young Man who Died*").

First and Second Bridesmaids. Miss Maude Millett and Miss Annie Hughes.

SCENE. — EMILY'S *Boudoir, sumptuously furnished
with a screen and sofa,* C. *Door,* R., *leading to*
EMILY'S *Bed-chamber. Door,* L. EMILY *discovered in loose wrapper, and reclining in uncomfort-
able position on sofa.*

EMILY (*dreamily*).   This day do I become the
    envied bride
Of Peter, justly surnamed Paragon ;
And much I wonder what in me he found
(He, who Perfection so personifies),
That he could condescend an eye to cast
On faulty feather-headed Emily !
How solemn is the stillness all around me !
           [*A loud bang is heard behind screen.*
Methought I heard the dropping of a pin ! —
Perhaps I should arise and search for it. . . .
Yet why, on second thoughts, disturb myself,
Since I am, by my settlements, to have
A handsome sum allowed for pin-money ?
Nay, since thou claim'st thy freedom, little pin,
I lack the heart to keep thee prisoner.
Go, then, and join the great majority
Of fallen, vagrant, unregarded pinhood —
My bliss is too supreme at such an hour
To heed such infidelities as thine.
           [*Falls into a happy revery.*

Enter FIRST *and* SECOND BRIDESMAIDS.

FIRST AND SECOND BRIDESMAIDS. What, how
    now, Emily — not yet attired?

Nay, haste, for Peter will be here anon!

[*They hurry her off by* R. *door, just as* PETER
    PARAGON *enters* L. *in bridal array.* N. B. — *The
    exigencies of the Drama are responsible for his
    making his appearance here, instead of waiting, as
    is more usual, at the church.*

PETER (*meditatively*). The golden sands of my
    celibacy

Are running low — soon falls the final grain!

Yet, even now, the glass I would not turn.

My Emily is not without her faults,

" *Was* not without them," I should rather say,

For during ten idyllic years of courtship,

By precept and example I have striven

To mould her to a helpmate fit for me.

Now, thank the gods, my labors are complete.

She stands redeemed from all her giddiness!

[*Here he steps upon the pin, and utters an excla-
    mation.*

Ha! What is this? I'm wounded . . . agony!

With what a darting pain my foot's transfixed!

I'll summon help (*with calm courage*) — yet, stay,
    I would not dim

This nuptial day by any sombre cloud.
I'll bear this stroke alone — and now to probe
The full extent of my calamity.

[*Seats himself on sofa in such a position as to be con-
     cealed by the screen from all but the audience, and
     proceeds to remove his boot.*

Ye powers of Perfidy, it is a pin!
I must know more of this — for it is meet
Such criminal neglect should be exposed.
Severe shall be that housemaid's punishment
Who's proved to be responsible for this!
But soft, I hear a step.

[*Enter* FIRST *and* SECOND BRIDESMAIDS, *who hunt
     diligently upon the carpet without observing* PETER'S
     presence.

EMILY'S VOICE (*within*).   Oh, search, I pray you.
It *must* be there — my own ears heard it fall!
                    [PETER *betrays growing uneasiness.*
THE BRIDESMAIDS.   Indeed, we fail to see it any-
          where!
EMILY (*entering distractedly in bridal costume, with
          a large rent in her train*).
You have no eyes, I tell you, let me help.
It must be found, or I am all undone!
In vain my cushion I have cut in two,

'Twas void of all but stuffing. .... Gracious Heavens,
To think that all my future bliss depends
On the evasive malice of a pin!

            [PETER *behind screen, starts violently.*
PETER (*aside*). A pin! what dire misgivings
      wring my heart!

[*Hops forward with a cold dignity, holding one foot
    in his hand.*

You seem in some excitement, Emily?
EMILY (*wildly*). *You*, Peter! . . . tell me —
      have you found a pin?
    PETER (*with deadly calm*). Unhappy girl —
      I *have!* (*To* BRIDESMAIDS.) Withdraw
      a while,
And should we need you we will summon you.

[*Exeunt* BRIDESMAIDS; EMILY *and* PETER *stand
    facing each other for some moments in dead
    silence.*

The pin is found — for I have trodden on it,
And may, for aught I know, be lamed for life.
Speak, Emily, what is that maid's desert
Whose carelessness has led to this mishap?
EMILY (*in the desperate hope of shielding herself*).
Why, should the fault be traced to any maid,

Instant dismissal shall be her reward,

With a month's wages paid in lieu of notice !

PETER (*with a passionless severity*).   From your
　　own lips I judge you, Emily.

Did they not own just now that you had heard

The falling of a pin — yet heeded not ?

Behold the outcome of your negligence !

　　　　　　　　　[*Extends his injured foot.*

EMILY.   Oh, let me kiss the place and make it
　　well !

PETER (*coldly withdrawing foot*).   Keep your
　　caresses till I ask for them.

My wound goes deeper than you wot of yet,

And by that disregarded pin is pricked

The iridescent bubble of Illusion !

EMILY (*slowly*).   Indeed, I do not wholly compre-
　　hend.

PETER.   Have patience, and I will be plainer yet.

Mine is a complex nature, Emily ;

Magnanimous, but still methodical.

An injury I freely can forgive,

Forget it (*striking his chest*), never !   She who
　　leaves about

Pins on the floor to pierce a lover's foot,

Will surely plant a thorn within the side

Of him whose fate it is to be her husband !

EMILY (*dragging herself towards him on her knees*). Have pity on me, Peter; I was mad !

PETER (*with emotion*). How can I choose but pity thee, poor soul,

Who, for the sake of temporary ease,

Hast forfeited the bliss that had been thine !

You could not stoop to pick a pin up. Why ?

Because, forsooth, 'twas but a paltry pin !

Yet, duly husbanded, that self-same pin

Had served you to secure your gaping train,

Your self-respect — and Me.

EMILY (*wailing*). What have I done ?

PETER. I will not now reproach you, Emily,

Nor would I dwell upon my wounded sole,

The pain of which increases momently.

I part from you in friendship, and in proof,

That fated instrument I leave with you

[*Presenting her with a pin, which she accepts mechanically.*

Which the frail link between us twain has severed.

I can dispense with it, for in my cuff

[*Shows her his coat-cuff, in which a row of pins'-heads is perceptible.*

I carry others 'gainst a time of need.

My poor success in life I trace to this

That never yet I passed a pin unheeded.

EMILY.   And is that all you have to say to me?

PETER.   I think so — save that I shall wish you
      well,

And pray that henceforth you may bear in mind ·

What vast importance lies in seeming trifles.

EMILY (*with a pale smile*).   Peter, your lesson
      is already learned,

For precious has this pin become for me,

Since by its aid I gain oblivion — thus!

[*Stabs herself.*

PETER (*coldly*).   Nay, these are histrionics, Emily.

[*Assists her to sofa.*

EMILY.   I'd skill enough to find a vital spot.

Do not withdraw it yet — my time is short,

And I have much to say before I die.

(*Faintly.*)   Be gentle with my rabbits when I'm
      gone ;

Give my canary chickweed now and then.

. . . I think there is no more — ah, one last word —

(*Earnestly*) — Warn them they must not cut our
      wedding-cake.

And then the pastrycook may take it back!

PETER (*Deeply moved*).   Would you had shown
      this thoughtfulness before !

[*Kneels by the sofa.*

EMILY.   'Tis now too late, and clearly do I see

That I was never worthy of you, Peter.

PETER *(gently)*.   'Tis not for me to contradict

    you now.

You did your best to be so, Emily !

EMILY.   A blessing on you for those generous

    words !

Now tell me, Peter, how is your poor foot ?

PETER.   The agony decidedly abates,

And I can almost bear a boot again.

EMILY.   Then I die happy ! . . . Kiss me, Peter

    . . . ah !   [*Dies.*

PETER.   In peace she passed away.   I'm glad

    of that,

Although that peace was purchased by a lie.

I shall not bear a boot for many days !

Thus ends our wedding morn, and she, poor child,

Has paid the penalty of heedlessness !

[*Curtain falls, whereupon, unless Mr. Punch is*
   greatly mistaken, there will not be a dry eye in the
   house.

V. — BRUNETTE AND BLANCHIDINE.

A MELODRAMATIC DIDACTIC VAUDEVILLE.

Suggested by " The Wooden Doll and the Wax Doll,"
by the Misses Jane and Ann Taylor.

DRAMATIS PERSONÆ.

BLANCHIDINE } By the celebrated Sisters STILTON, the
BRUNETTE. } Champion Duettists and Clog-Dancers.

FANNY FURBELOW. By MISS SYLVIA SEALSKIN (*by kind
permission of* THE GAYETY MANAGEMENT).

FRANK MANLY. By Mr. HENRY NEVILLE.

SCENE. — *A sunny Glade in Kensington Gardens,
between the Serpentine and Round Pond.*

Enter BLANCHIDINE *and* BRUNETTE, *with their
arms thrown affectionately around one another.*
BLANCHIDINE *is carrying a large and expression-
less wooden doll.*

Duet and Step-dance.

BL. Oh, I do adore Brunette! (*Dances.*) Tippity-tappity, tappity-tippity, tippity-tappity,
tip-tap !

BR. Blanchidine's the sweetest pet! (*Dances.*)
    Tippity-tappity, etc.

TOGETHER.

> When the sun is high,
> We come out to ply,
> Nobody is nigh,
> All is mirth and j'y !
> With a pairosol,
> We'll protect our doll,
> Make a mossy bed
> For her wooden head!

[*Combination step-dance, during which both watch their feet with an air of detached and slightly amused interest, as if they belonged to some other persons.*

Clickity-clack, clickity-clack, clickity, clickity, clickity-clack; clackity-clickity, clickity-clackity, clackity-clickity-*clack!*

> [*Repeat ad. lib.*

BL. (*apologetically to audience*). Her taste in dress is rather plain! (*Dances.*) Tippity-tappity, etc.

BR. (*in pitying aside*). It *is* a pity she's so vain! (*Dances.*) Tippity-tappity, etc.

BL.   'Tis a shime to smoile,

           But she's shocking stoyle,

           It is quite a troyal,

           Still — she mikes a foil !

BR.   Often I've a job

           To suppress a sob,

           She is such a snob,

           When she meets a nob !

                          [*Step-dance as before.*

[*N. B. — In consideration of the well-known difficulty that most popular Variety-Artists experience
in the metrical delivery of decasyllabic couplets,
the lines which follow have been written as they
will most probably be spoken.*

BL. (*looking off with alarm.*) Why, here comes
    Fanny Furbelow, a new frock from Paris
    in !

She'll find me with Brunette — it's *too* embar-
    rassing !

                           [*Aside.*

(*To* BRUNETTE.) Brunette, my love, I know *such*
    a pretty game we'll play at —

Poor Timburina's ill, and the seaside she ought
    to stay at.

(The Serpentine's the seaside, let's pretend.)
And *you* shall take her there — (*hypocritically*)
 — you're such a friend !

Br. (*with simplicity*). Oh, yes, that *will* be
  splendid, Blanchidine,

And then we can go and have a dip in a bathing-
  machine !

[Blan. *resigns the wooden doll to* Brun., *who skips
  off with it,* l., *as* Fanny Furbelow *enters* r.,
  carrying a magnificent wax doll.

Fanny (*languidly*). Ah, howdy do — *isn't* this
  heat too frightful ? And so you're quite
  alone?

Bl. (*nervously*). Oh, *quite* — oh yes, I always
  am alone, when there's nobody with me.

[*This is a little specimen of the Lady's humorous
  "gag," at which she is justly considered a pro-
  ficient.*

Fanny (*drawling*).   Delightful !
When I was wondering, only a little while ago,
If I should meet a creature that I know ;
Allow me — my new doll, the Lady Minnie !

                        [*Introducing doll.*

Bl. (*rapturously*). Oh, what a perfect love !
Fanny.   She ought to be — for a guinea !

Here, you may nurse her for a little while.
Be careful, for her frock's the latest style. ·

> [*Gives* BLAN. *the wax doll.*

She's the best wax, and has three changes of cloth-
    ing —
For those cheap wooden dolls I've quite a loathing.

BL. (*hastily*).   Oh, so have *I*— they're not to be
    endured!

Re-enter BRUNETTE *with the wooden doll, which she
    tries to press upon* BLANCHIDINE, *much to the
    latter's confusion.*

BR.   I've brought poor Timburina back, com-
    pletely cured!
Why, aren't you pleased?   Your face is looking *so*
    cloudy!

F. (*haughtily*).   Is she a friend of *yours* — this
    little dowdy?   [*Slow music.*

BL. (*after an internal struggle*).   Oh, no, what an
    idea!
Why, I don't even know her by name!
Some vulgar child. . . .

> [*Lets the wax doll fall unregarded on the gravel.*

BR. (*indignantly*).   Oh, what a horrid shame!
I see *now* why you sent us to the Serpentine!

BL. (*heartlessly*).   There's no occasion to flare up
    like turpentine.

Br. (*ungrammatically*). I'm *not!* Disown your
    doll, and thrust me, too, aside!

The one thing left for both of us is — suicide!

Yes, Timburina, us no more she cherishes —

(*Bitterly*). Well, the Round Pond a handy place
    to perish is!

                  [*Rushes off stage with wooden doll.*

Bl. (*making a feeble attempt to follow*). Come
    back, Brunette; don't leave me thus, in
    charity!

F. (*with contempt*). Well, I'll be off — since you
    seem to prefer vulgarity.

Bl. No, stay — but — ah, she said — what if she
    meant it?

F. Not she! And, if she did, *we* can't prevent it.

Bl. (*relieved*). That's true — we'll play, and think
    no more about her.

F. (*sarcastically*). We may *just* manage to get on
    without her!

So come — (*Perceives doll lying face upwards on
    path.*)

You odious girl, what have you done?

Left Lady Minnie lying in the blazing sun!

'Twas done on purpose — oh, you *thing* perfidious!

                  [*Stamps.*

You *knew* she'd melt, and get completely hideous!

Don't answer *me*, Miss — I wish we'd never met.
You're only fit for persons like Brunette!

[*Picks up doll, and exit in passion.*

Grand Sensation Descriptive Soliloquy, by BLANCH-
IDINE, *to Melodramatic Music.*

BL.   Gone! Ah, I am rightly punished! What
would I not give now to have homely little Brunette, and dear old wooden-headed Timburina back
again! *She* wouldn't melt in the sun. . . . Where
are they now?   Great Heavens! that threat — that
rash resolve. . . . I remember all! 'Twas in the
direction of the Pond they vanished. (*Peeping
anxiously between trees.*)   Are they still in sight?
. . . Yes, I see them.   Brunette has reached the
water's edge. . . . What is she purposing?   Now
she kneels on the rough gravel; she is making
Timburina kneel too!   How calm and resolute they
both appear!   (*Shuddering.*)   I dare not look
further — but ah, I must — *I must!* . . . Horror!
I saw her boots flash for an instant in the bright
sunlight: and now the ripples have closed, smiling,
over her little black stockings! . . . Help! — save
her, somebody! — help!. . . . Joy! a gentleman
has appeared on the scene — how handsome, how
brave he looks!   He has taken in the situation at

a glance! With quiet composure he removes his coat — oh, *don't* trouble about folding it up! — and why, *why* remove your gloves, when there is not a moment to be lost? Now, with many injunctions, he entrusts his watch to a bystander, who retires, overcome by emotion. And now — oh, gallant, heroic soul! — now he is sending his toy-terrier into the seething water. (*Straining eagerly forward.*) Ah, the dog paddles bravely out — he has reached the spot . . . oh, he has passed it! — he is trying to catch a duck! Dog, dog, *is* this a time for pursuing ducks? At last he understands — he dives . . . he brings up — agony! a small tin cup! Again . . . *this* time, surely — what, only an old pot-hat! . . . Oh, this dog is a fool! And still the Round Pond holds its dread secret! Once more . . . yes — no, yes, it *is* Timburina! Thank Heaven, she yet breathes! But Brunette? Can she have stuck in the mud at the bottom? Ha, she, too, is rescued — saved — ha-ha-ha! — saved, saved, saved!

[*Swoons hysterically amid deafening applause.*

Enter FRANK MANLY *supporting* BRUNETTE, *who carries* TIMBURINA.

BL. (*wildly*). What, do I see you safe, beloved Brunette?

Br. Yes, thanks to his courage, I'm not even *wet!*

Frank (*modestly*). Nay, spare your compliments.
    To rescue Beauty,
When in distress, is every hero's duty!

Bl. Brunette, forgive — I'm cured of all my folly!

Br. (*heartily*). Of course I will, my dear, and so
    will dolly!

[*Grand Trio and Step-dance, with "tippity-tappity,"*
    and " clickity-clack " refrain as finale.

VI. — COMING OF AGE.

OUR present Drama represents an attempt to illustrate upon the Music-hall stage the eternal truth that race *will* tell in the long run, despite — but, on second thoughts, it does not *quite* prove that, though it certainly shows the unerring accuracy of parental — at least, that is not exactly its tendency, either; and the fact is that *Mr. Punch* is more than a little mixed himself as to the precise theory which it is designed to enforce. He hopes, however, that, as a realistic study of Patrician life and manners, it will possess charms for a democratic audience.

COMING OF AGE.

A GRAND SOCIAL PSYCHOLOGICAL COMEDY-DRAMA IN ONE ACT.

DRAMATIS PERSONÆ.

THE EARL OF BURNTALMOND.

THE COUNTESS OF BURNTALMOND (*his wife*).

ROBERT HENRY VISCOUNT BULLSAYE (*their son and heir*).

THE LADY ROSE CARAMEL (*niece to the Earl*).

HOREHOUND . .	Travelling as "The Celebrated Combination Korffdropp Troupe," in their refined and elegant Drawing-room Entertainment.
MRS. HOREHOUND .	
COLTSFOOT HOREHOUND	

TENANTRY.

SCENE. — *The Great Quadrangle of Hardbake Cas-*
tle; banners, mottoes, decorations, etc.   On the
steps, R., *the* EARL, *supported by his wife, son,*
and niece, is discovered in the act of concluding a
speech to six tenantry, who display all the enthu-
siasm that is reasonably to be expected at ninepence
a night.

THE EARL (*patting* LORD BULLSAYE'S *shoulder*).
I might say more, gentlemen, in praise of my dear
son, Lord Bullsaye, here — I might dwell on his
extreme sweetness, his strongly marked character,
the variety of his tastes, and the singular attraction
he has for children of all ages — but I forbear.   I
will merely announce that on this day — the day
he has selected for attaining his majority — he has
gratified us all by plighting troth to his cousin, the
Lady Rose Caramel, with whose dulcet and cling-
ing disposition he has always possessed the greatest
natural affinity.   [*Cheers.*

LORD BULLSAYE (*aside to* LADY R.).   Ah, Rose,
would such happiness could last!   But my heart
misgives me strangely — why, I know not.

LADY R.   Say not so, dear Bullsaye — have you
not just rendered me the happiest little Patrician
in the whole peerage?

LORD B. 'Tis true — and yet, and yet — pooh, let me snatch the present hour!   [*Snatches it.*

THE EARL. And now, let the Revels commence.

Enter the KORFFDROPP TROUPE, *who give their marvellous Entertainment, entitled, " The Three Surprise Packets ; " after which —*

HOREHOUND. This will conclude the first portion of our Entertainment, Lords, Ladies, *and* Gentlemen ; and, while my wife and pardner retires to change her costoom for the Second Part, I should be glad of the hoppertoonity of a short pussonal hexplanation with the noble Herl on my right.   [*Exit* MRS. HOREHOUND.

THE EARL (*graciously*). I will hear you, fellow ! (*Aside.*) Strange how familiar his features seem to me !

HOREH. The fact is, your Lordship's celebrating the coming of hage of the *wrong heir.* (*Sensation — i.e., the six tenantry shift from one leg to the other, and murmur feebly.*) Oh, I can prove it. Twenty-one years ago — (*slow music*) — I was in your Lordship's service as gamekeeper, 'ead whip, and hextry waiter. My son and yours was born the self-same day, and my hold dutch was selected to hact as foster-mother to the youthful lord. Well

— (*tells a long, and not entirely original, story ; marvellous resemblance between infants, only distinguishable by green and magenta bows, etc., etc.*), soon after, your Lordship discharged me at a moment's notice —

THE EARL (*haughtily*). I did, upon discovering that you were in the habit of surreptitiously carrying off kitchen-stuff, concealed within your umbrella. But proceed with your narration.

HOREH. I swore to be avenged, and so — (*common form again; the shifted bows*) — consequently, as a moment's reflection will convince you, the young man on the steps, in the button-'ole and tall 'at, is my lawful son, while the real Viscount is — (*presenting* COLTSFOOT, *who advances modestly on his hands*) — 'ere !

[*Renewed sensation.*

THE EARL. This is indeed a startling piece of intelligence. (*To* LORD B.) And so, sir, it appears that your whole life has been one consistent imposition — a gilded *lie ?*

LORD B. Let my youth and inexperience at the time, sir, plead as my best excuse !

THE E. Nothing can excuse the fact that you — you, a low-born son of the people, have monopolized the training, the tenderness and education, which were the due of your Patrician foster-brother. (*To* COLTSFOOT.) Approach, my injured, long-lost boy, and tell me how I may atone for these years of injustice and neglect!

COLTS. Well, Guv'nor, if you send out for a pot o' four arf, it 'ud be a *beginning*, like.

THE E. You shall have every luxury that befits your rank, but first remove that incongruous garb.

COLTS. (*To* LORD B.). These 'ere togs belong to *you* now, young feller, and I reckon exchange ain't no robbery.

LORD B. (*with emotion to* COUNTESS). Mother, can you endure to behold your son in tights and spangles on the very day of his majority?

COUNTESS (*coldly*). On the contrary, it is my wish to see him attired as soon as possible in a more appropriate costume.

LORD B. (*to* LADY R.). Rose, *you*, at least, have not changed? Tell me you will love me still, even on the precarious summit of an acrobat's pole!

LADY ROSE (*scornfully*). Really, the presumptuous familiarity of the lower orders is perfectly appalling!

THE EARL (*to* COUNTESS, *as* LORD B. *and* COLTSFOOT *retire to exchange costumes*). At last, Pauline, I understand why I could never feel towards Bullsaye the affection of a parent. Often have I reproached myself for a coldness I could not overcome.

COUNTESS. And I too! Nature was too strong for us. But, oh, the joy of recovering our son — of finding him so strong, so supple, so agile. Never yet has our line boasted an heir who can feed himself from a fork strapped onto his dexter heel!

THE E. (*with emotion*). Our beloved, boneless boy!

[*Re-enter* COLTSFOOT *in modern dress, and* LORD B. *in tights.*

COLTS. Don't I look slap up — O. K. and no mistake? Oh, I *am* 'aving a beano!

ALL. What easy gayety and unforced animation!

THE E. My dear boy, let me present you to your *fiancée*. Rose, my love, this is your *legitimate* lover.

COLTS. Oh, all right, *I've* no objections — on'y there'll be ructions with the young woman in the tight-rope line as I've been keepin' comp'ny with — that's all!

THE E. Your foster-brother will act as your

substitute there. (*Proudly.*) *My* son must make no *mésalliance !*

Rose (*timidly*). And, if it would give you any pleasure, I'm sure I could soon learn the tight-rope!

Colts. Not at *your* time o' life, Miss, and besides, 'ang it, now I'm a lord, I can't have my wife doin' nothing low!

The E. Spoken like a true Burntalmond! And now let the Revels recommence.

[*Re-enter* Mrs. Horehound.

Horeh. (*to* Lord B.). Now then, stoopid, tumble, can't you — what are you 'ere *for?*

Lord B. (*to the* Earl). Since it is your command, I obey, though it is ill tumbling with a heavy heart! [*Turns head over heels laboriously.*

Colts. Call *that* a somersault? 'Ere, 'old my 'at (*giving tall hat to* Lady R.) *I'll* show yer 'ow to do a turn. [*Throws a triple somersault.*

All. What condescension! How his aristo-cratic superiority is betrayed, even in competition with those to the manner born!

Mrs. Horeh. (*still in ignorance of the trans-formation*). Halt! I have kept silence till now — even from my husband, but the time has come when I *must* speak. Think you that if he were indeed a lord, he could turn such somersaults as those? No — no I will reveal all. (*Tells same old story — except that she herself from ambitious motives transposed the infants' bows*). Now, do with me what you will!

HOREH.   Confusion, so my ill-judged action did but redress the wrong I designed to effect!

THE E. (*annoyed*).   This is a serious matter, reflecting as it does upon the legitimacy of my lately recovered son.   What proof have you, woman, of your preposterous allegation?

MRS. H.   None, my lord, — but these —

[*Exhibits two faded bunches of ribbon.*

THE E.   I cannot resist such overwhelming evidence, fight against it as I may.

LORD B. (*triumphantly*).   And so — oh, Father, Mother, Rose — dear, dear Rose — I am no acrobat, after all!·

THE E. (*sternly*).   Would you were anything half so serviceable to the community, sir!   I have no superstitious reverence for rank, and am, I trust, sufficiently enlightened to discern worth and merit — even beneath the spangled vest of the humblest acrobat.   Your foster-brother, brief as our acquaintance has been, has already endeared himself to all hearts, while you have borne a

trifling reverse of fortune with sullen discontent
and conspicuous incapacity. He has perfected
himself in a lofty and distinguished profession
during years spent by *you*, sir, in idly cumbering
the earth of Eton and Oxford. Shall I allow him
to suffer by a purely accidental coincidence?
Never! I owe him reparation, and it shall be paid
to the uttermost penny. From this day I adopt
him as my eldest son, and the heir to my earldom,
and all other real and personal effects. See,
Robert Henry, that you treat your foster-brother
as your senior in future!

COLTS. (*to* LORD B.). Way-oh, ole matey, I
don't bear no malice, *I* don't! Give us your dooks.

[*Offering hand.*

THE C. Ah, Bullsaye, try to be worthy of such
generosity!

[LORD B. *grasps* COLTSFOOT'S *hand in silence.*

LADY ROSE. And pray, understand that,
whether Mr. Coltsfoot be viscount or acrobat,
it can make no difference whatever to the disinterested affection with which I have lately
learnt to regard him.

[*Gives her hand to* COLTSFOOT, *who squeezes it with
ardor.*

COLTS. (*pleasantly*). Well, Father, Mother,

your noble Herlship and Lady, foster-brother
Bullsaye, and my pretty little sweet'art 'ere, what
do you all say to goin' inside and shunting a little
garbage, and shifting a drop or so of lotion, eh?

THE E. A most sensible suggestion, my boy.
Let us make these ancient walls the scene of the
blithest — ahem! — *beano* they have ever yet
beheld!

Cheers from tenantry, as the EARL *leads the way
into the Castle with* MRS. HOREHOUND, *followed
by* HOREHOUND *with the* COUNTESS *and* COLTS-
FOOT *with* LADY ROSE, LORD BULLSAYE, *dis-
comfited and abashed, entering last as Curtain
falls.*

VII. — RECLAIMED;

OR, HOW LITTLE ELFIE TAUGHT HER GRAND-MOTHER.

CHARACTERS.

LADY BELLEDAME (*a Dowager of the deepest dye*).

MONKSHOOD (*her Steward and confidential Minion*).

LITTLE ELFIE (*an Angel Child*). This part has been specially constructed for that celebrated Infant Actress, Banjoist, and Variety Comédienne, MISS BIRDIE CALLOWCHICK.

SCENE — *The Panelled Room at Nightshade Hall.*

LADY BELLEDAME (*discovered preparing parcels*). Old and unloved! — yes the longer I live, the more plainly do I perceive that I am *not* a popular old woman. Have I not acquired the reputation in the county of being a witch? My neighbor, Sir Vevey Long, asked me publicly only the other day " when I would like my broom ordered," and that minx, Lady Violet Powdray, has pointedly mentioned old cats in my hearing! Pergament, my family lawyer, has declined to act for me any longer, merely because Monkshood rack-rented some of the tenants a little too energetically in the Torture Chamber — as if in these hard times one was not justified in putting the screw on! Then the villagers scowl when I pass; the very children shrink from me — [*A childish voice outside window*, "Yah, 'oo sold 'erself to Old Bogie for a pound o' tea an' a set o' noo teeth?"] — that is, when they do not insult me by suggestions of bargains that are not even businesslike! No matter — I will be avenged upon them all — ay, all! 'Tis Christmas-time — the season at which sentimental fools exchange gifts and good wishes. For once I, too, will distribute a few seasonable presents. . . . (*Inspecting parcels.*) Are my arrangements complete? The bundle of choice cigars, in each of which a charge of nitro-glycerine has been dexterously inserted? The lip-salve, made up from my own prescription with corrosive sublimate by a venal chemist in the vicinity? The art flower-pot, containing a fine specimen of the Upas plant, swathed in impermeable sacking? The sweets compounded with sugar of lead? The packet of best ratsbane? Yes, nothing has been omitted. Now to summon my faithful Monkshood. . . . Ha! he is already at hand.

[*Chord as* MONKSHOOD *enters.*

MONKSHOOD.   Your Ladyship, a child, whose

sole luggage is a small bandbox and a large banjo, is without, and requests the favor of a personal interview.

LADY B. (*reproachfully*). And you, who have been with me all these years, and know my ways, omitted to let loose the bloodhounds? You grow careless, Monkshood!

MONKS. (*wounded*). Your Ladyship is unjust — I *did* unloose the bloodhounds; but the ferocious animals merely sat up and begged. The child had took the precaution to provide herself with a bun!

LADY B. No matter, she must be removed — I care not how.

MONKS. There may be room for one more — a little one — in the old well. The child mentioned that she was your Ladyship's granddaughter, but I presume that will make no difference?

LADY B. (*disquieted*). What! — then she must be the child of my only son Poldoodle, whom, for refusing to cut off the entail, I had falsely accused of adulterating milk, and transported beyond the seas! She comes hither to denounce and reproach me! Monkshood, she must not leave this place alive — you hear?

MONKS. I require no second bidding — ha, the child . . . she comes!

[*Chord. Little* ELFIE *trips in with touching self-confidence.*

ELFIE (*in a charming little Cockney accent*). Yes, Grandma, it's me — little Elfie, come all the way from Australia to see you, because I thought you must be sow lownly all by yourself! My Papa often told me what a long score he owed you, and how he hoped to pay you off if he lived. But he went out to business one day — Pa was a bush-ranger, you know, and worked — oh, *so* hard; and never came back to his little Elfie, so poor little Elfie has come to live with you!

MONKS. Will you have the child removed now, my Lady?

LADY B. (*undecidedly*). Not now — not yet; I have other work for you. These Christmas gifts, to be distributed amongst my good friends and neighbors (*handing parcels*). First, this bundle of cigars to Sir Vevey Long, with my best wishes that such a connoisseur in tobacco may find them sufficiently strong. The salve for Lady Violet Powdray, with my love, and it should be rubbed on the last thing at night. The plant you will take to the little Pergaments — 'twill serve them for a Christmas tree. This packet to be diluted in a barrel of beer, which you will see broached upon the village green ; these sweetmeats for distribution among the most deserving of the school-children.

ELFIE (*throwing her arms around* LADY B.'s *neck*). I *do* like you, Grandma, you have such a kind face! And oh, what pains you must have taken to find something that will do for everybody!

LADY B. (*disengaging herself peevishly*). Yes, yes, child. I trust that what I have chosen will indeed do for everybody, — but I do not like to be messed about. Monkshood, you know what you have to do.

ELFIE. Oh, I am sure he does, Grandma! See how benevolently he smiles. You're such a good old man, you will take care that all the poor people are fed, *won't* you?

MONKS. (*with a sinister smile*). Ah! Missie, I've 'elped to settle a many people's 'ash in my time!

ELFIE (*innocently*). What, do they all get hash? How nice! I like hash, — but what else do you give them?

MONKS. (*grimly*). Gruel, Missie. (*Aside.*) I must get out of this, or this innocent child's prattle will unman me! [*Exit with parcels.*

ELFIE. You seem so sad and troubled, Grandma. Let me sing you one of the songs with which I drew a smile from poor dear Pa in happier days.

LADY B.   No, no, some other time. (*Aside.*) Pshaw! why should I dread the effect of her simple melodies? (*Aloud.*) Sing, child, if you will.

ELFIE.   How glad I am that I brought my banjo!   [*Sings.*

Dar is a lubly yaller gal dat tickles me to deff;
She'll dance de room ob darkies down, and take away
      deir breff.
When she sits down to supper, ebery colored gemple-
      man,
As she gets her upper lip o'er a plate o' "possom
      dip," cries,
" Woa, Lucindy Ann!"   (Chorus, dear Granny!)

Chorus.

Woa, Lucindy!   Woa, Lucindy!   Woa, Lucindy
      Ann!
At de rate dat you are stuffin, you will nebber leave
      us nuffin; so woa, Miss Sindy Ann!

To LADY B. (*who, after joining in chorus with deep emotion, has burst into tears*). Why, you are *weeping*, dear Grandmother!

LADY B. Nay, 'tis nothing, child — but have you no songs which are less sad?

ELFIE. Oh, yes, I know plenty of plantation ditties more cheerful than that. (*Sings.*)

Oh, I hear a gentle whisper from de days ob long ago,
When I used to be a happy darkie slave.
　　　　　　　　[*Trump-a-trump!*
But now I'se got to labor wif the shovel an' de hoe —
For ole Massa lies a sleepin' in his grave!
　　　　　　　　[*Trump-trump!*
　　　　Chorus.
Poor ole Massa! Poor ole Massa! (Pianissimo.)
　　Poor ole Massa, that I nebber more shall see!
He was let off by de jury, Way down in old Missouri
　　— But dey lynched him on a persimmon-tree.

ELFIE. You smile at last, dear Grandma! I would sing to you again, but I am so very, very sleepy!

LADY B. Poor child, you have had a long journey. Rest a while on this couch, and I will arrange this screen so as to protect your slumbers.
　　　　　　　　　[*Leads little* ELFIE *to couch.*

ELFIE (*sleepily*). Thanks, dear Grandma, thanks. . . . Now I shall go to sleep, and dream of you, and the dogs, and angels. I so often dream about angels — but that is generally after supper, and to-night I have had no supper. . . . But never mind. . . . Good-night, Grannie, good-night . . . goo'ni' . . . goo . . . goo!

[*She sinks softly to sleep.*

LADY B. And I was about to set the blood-hounds upon this little sunbeam! 'Tis long since these grim walls have echoed strains so sweet as hers. (*Croons.*) "Woa, Lucindy," etc. "Dey tried him by a Jury, way down in ole Missouri, an' dey hung him to a possumdip tree!" (*Goes to couch, and gazes on the little sleeper.*) How peacefully she slumbers! What a change has come over me in one short hour! — my withered heart is sending up green shoots of tenderness, of love, and hope! Let me try henceforth to be worthy of this dear child's affection and respect. (*Turns, and sees* MONKSHOOD.) Ha, Monkshood! Then there is time yet! Those parcels . . . quick, quick! — the parcels! —

MONKS. (*impassively*). Have been left as you instructed, my Lady.

[*Chord.* LADY B. *staggers back, gasping, into chair. Little* ELFIE *awakes behind screen, and rubs her eyes.*

LADY B. (*in a hoarse whisper*). You — you have left the parcels . . . all — *all?* Tell me — how

were they received? Speak low — I would not
that yonder child should awake and hear!

LITTLE ELFIE (*behind the screen, very wide awake,
indeed*). Dear, good old Grannie — she would
conceal her generosity — even from *me!* (*Loudly.*)
She little thinks that I am overhearing all!

MONKS. I could have sworn I heard whispering.

LADY B. Nay, you are mistaken — 'twas but
the wind in the old wainscot. (*Aside.*) He is
quite capable of destroying that innocent child;
but old and attached servant as he is, there are
liberties I still know how to forbid. (*To* M). Your
story — quick!

MONKS. First, I delivered the cigars to Sir
Vevey Long, whom I found under his veranda.
He seemed surprised and gratified by the gift,
selected a weed, and was proceeding to light it,
whilst he showed a desire to converse familiarly
with me. 'Astily excusing myself, I drove away,
when —

LADY B. When *what?* Do not torture a
wretched old woman!

MONKS. When I heard a loud report behind
me, and, in the portion of a brace, two waistcoat-
buttons, and half a slipper, which hurtled past my
ears, I recognized all that was mortal of the late

Sir Vevey. You mixed them cigars uncommon strong, m'Lady.

Elfie (*aside*). Can it be? But no, no. I will *not* believe it. I am sure that dear Granny meant no harm!

Lady B. (*with a grim pride she cannot wholly repress*). I have devoted some study to the subject of explosives. 'Tis another triumph to the Anti-tobacconists. And what of Lady Violet Powdray — did she apply the salve?

Monks. Judging from the 'eartrending 'owls which proceeded from Carmine Cottage, the salve was producing the desired result. Her Ladyship, 'owever, terminated her sufferings somewhat pre-matoor by jumping out of a top winder just as I was taking my departure —

Lady B. She should have died hereafter — but no matter . . . and the Upas-tree? —

Monks. Was presented to the Pergaments, who unpacked it, and loaded its branches with toys and tapers; after which Mr. Pergament, Mrs. P., and all the little Pergaments joined 'ands, and danced round it in light'arted glee. (*In a sombre tone.*) They little knoo as how it was their dance of death!

Lady B. That knowledge will come! And the beer, Monkshood — you saw it broached?

MONKS. Upon the village green ; the mortality is still spreading, it being found impossible to undo the knots in which the victims have tied themselves. The sweetmeats likewise were distributed, and the floor of the hinfant-school now resembles one vast fly-paper.

LADY B. (*with a touch of remorse*). The children too ! Was not my little Elfie once an infant? Ah me, ah me !

ELFIE (*aside*). Once — but that was long, long ago. And, oh, *how* disappointed I am in poor dear Grandmamma!

LADY B. Monkshood, you should not have done these things — you should have saved me from myself. You *must* have known how greatly all this would increase my unpopularity in the neighborhood.

MONKS. (*sulkily*). And this is my reward for obeying orders! Take care, my Lady. It suits you now to throw me aside like a — (*casting about for an original simile*) — like a old glove, because this innocent grandchild of yours has touched your flinty 'art. But where will *you* be when she learns ? —

LADY B. (*in agony*). Ah, no, Monkshood, good, faithful Monkshood, she must never know that!

Think, Monkshood, you would not tell her that the Grandmother to whom she looks up with such touching, childlike love, was a — *homicide* — you would not do that?

MONKS. Some would say even 'omicide was not too black a name for all you've done. (LADY BELLEDAME *shudders*.) I might tell Miss Elfie how you've blowed up a live Baronet, corrosive sublimated a gentle Lady, honly for 'aving, in a moment of candor, called you a hold cat, and distributed pison in a variety of forms about this smiling village; and if that don't inspire her with distrust, I don't know the nature of children, that's all! I might tell her, I say, and, if I'm to keep my mouth shut, I shall expect it to be considered in my wages.

LADY B. I knew you had a good heart! I will pay you anything — anything provided you shield my guilt from her . . . wait, you shall have gold, gold, Monkshood, gold!

[*Chord. Little* ELFIE *suddenly comes from behind screen; limelight on her. The other two shrink back.*

ELFIE. Do not give that bad old man money, Grandmother, for it will only be wasted.

LADY B. Speak, child! — how much do you know?

ELFIE. All!

> [*Chord.* LADY B. *collapses on chair.*

LADY B. (*with an effort*). And now, Elfie, that you know, you scorn and hate your poor old Grandmother — is it not so?

ELFIE. It is wrong to hate one's Grandmother, whatever she does. At first when I heard, I was very, very sorry. I *did* think it was most unkind of you. But now, oh, I *can't* believe that you had not some good, wise motive, in acting as you did!

LADY B. (*in conscience-stricken aside*). Even *this* cannot shatter her artless faith. . . . Oh, wretch, wretch!   [*Covers her face.*

MONKS. Motive — I believe you there, Missie. Why, she went and insured all their lives afore-hand, *she* did.

LADY B. Monkshood, in pity hold your peace!

ELFIE (*her face beaming*). I knew it — I was sure of it! Oh, Granny, my dear, kind old Granny, you insured their lives first, so that no real harm could possibly happen to them — oh, I am so happy!

LADY B. (*aside*). What shall I say? Merciful Powers, what *shall* I say to her?

> [*Disturbed sounds without.*

MONKS. I don't know what you'd better *say*, but I can tell you what your Ladyship had better *do* — and that is, take your 'ook while you can. Even now the outraged populace approaches, to wreak a hawful vengeance upon your guilty 'ed!

[*Melodramatic music.*

LADY B. (*distractedly*). A mob! I cannot face them — they will tear me limb from limb. At my age I could not survive such an indignity as that! Hide me, Monkshood — help me to escape!

MONKS. There is a secret underground passage, known only to myself, communicating with the nearest railway station. I will point it out, and personally conduct your Ladyship — for a consideration — one thousand pounds down.

[*The noise increases.*

ELFIE. No, Granny, don't trust him! Be calm and brave. Await the mob here. Leave it all to me. I will explain everything to them — how you meant no ill, — how, at the very time they thought you were meditating an injury, you were actually spending money in insuring all their lives. When I tell them *that* —

MONKS. Ah, you tell 'em that, and see. It's too late now — they are here!

[*Shouts without.* LADY B. *crouches on floor.
Little* ELFIE *goes to the window, throws open the
shutters, and stands on balcony in her fluttering
white robe and the limelight.*

ELFIE. Yes, they are here. Why, they are
carrying torches! — (LADY B. *groans*) — and banners, too! I think they have a band. . . . Who is
that tall, stout gentleman, in the white hat, on
horseback, and the lady in a pony-trap, with, oh,
such a beautiful complexion! There is an inscription on one of the flags — I can read it quite
plainly, " *Thanks to the generous Donor !* " (That
must be *you*, Grandmother!) And there are children who dance, and scatter flowers. They are asking for a speech. (*Speaking off.*) " If you please,
Ladies and Gentlemen, my Grandmamma is not at
all well, but she wishes me to say she wishes you
a Merry Christmas, and is very glad you all like
your presents so much. Good-by, *good*-by ! "
(*Returning down Stage.*) Now they have gone
away, Granny. . . . They did look so grateful!

LADY B. (*bewildered*). What is this! Sir
Vevey, Lady Violet, — alive, well? This deputa-
tion of gratitude? Am I mad, dreaming — or
what does it all mean?

MONKS. (*doggedly*). It means that the sight of

this 'ere angel child recalled me to a sense of what I might be exposin' myself to by carrying out your Ladyship's commands; and so I took the liberty of substitootin gifts more calculated to inspire gratitude in their recipients — that's what it means.

LADY B. Wretch! — then you have disobeyed me? You leave this day month!

ELFIE (*pleadingly*). Nay, Grandmother, bear with him, for has not his disobedience spared you from acts that you might some day have regretted? . . . There, Mr. Butler, Granny forgives you — see, she holds out her hand, and here's mine; and now —

LADY B. (*smiling tenderly*). Now you shall sing us " *Woa Lucinda !* "

[*Little* ELFIE *fetches her banjo, and sings, " Woa, Lucinda!" her* GRANDMOTHER *and the aged* STEWARD, *joining in the dance and chorus, and embracing the child, to form picture as Curtain falls.*

VIII.—JACK PARKER;

OR, THE BULL WHO KNEW HIS BUSINESS.

CHARACTERS.

JACK PARKER ("*was a cruel boy, For mischief was his sole employ.*" — *Vide* MISS JANE TAYLOR.)

MISS LYDIA BANKS ("*though very young, Will never do what's rude or wrong.*" — *Ditto.*)

FARMER BANKS. . . } By the Brothers GRIFFITHS.
FARMER BANKS'S BULL }

Chorus of Farm-Hands.

SCENE. — *A farmyard.* R. *a stall from which the head of the Bull is visible above the half-door. Enter* FARMER BANKS *with a cudgel.*

FARMER B. (*moodily*). When roots are quiet, and cereals are dull,

I vent my irritation on the Bull.

[*We have* MISS TAYLOR'S *own authority for this rhyme.*

Come hup, you beast!

[*Opens stall and flourishes cudgel. The Bull comes forward with an air of deliberate defiance.*

169

Oh, turning nasty, is he?

[*Apologetically to Bull.*

Another time will do!   I see you're busy!

[*The Bull, after some consideration, decides to accept this retractation, and retreats with dignity to his stall, the door of which he carefully fastens after him. Exit* FARMER BANKS, L., *as* LYDIA BANKS *enters* R. *accompanied by Chorus. The Bull exhibits the liveliest interest in her proceedings, as he looks on, with his forelegs folded easily upon the top of the door.*

Song. — LYDIA BANKS (*in Polka time*).

I'm the child by Miss Jane Taylor sung;
Unnaturally good for one so young —
A pattern for the people that I go among,
With my moral little tags on the tip of my tongue.
And I often feel afraid that I sha'n't live long,
For I never do a thing that's rude or wrong!
Chorus (*to which the Bull beats time*).   As a general
    rule, one *doesn't* live long,
If you never do a thing that's rude or wrong!

Second Verse.

My words are all with wisdom fraught,
To make polite replies I've sought;

And learned by independent thought,
That a pinafore, inked, is good for nought.
So wonderfully well have I been taught,
That I turn my toes as children ought!

Chorus (to which the Bull dances). This moral
    lesson she's been taught —
She turns her toes as children ought!
LYDIA *(sweetly).* Yes, I'm the Farmer's daughter
    — Lydia Banks;
No person ever caught me playing pranks!
I'm loved by all the live-stock on the farm,

        [Ironical applause from the Bull.

Pigeons I've plucked will perch upon my arm,
And pigs at my approach sit up and beg.

        [Business by Bull.

For me the partial peacock saves his egg,
No sheep e'er snaps if *I* attempt to touch her,
Lambs *like* it when I lead them to the butcher!
Each morn I milk my rams beneath the shed,
While rabbits flutter twittering round my head,
And, as befits a dairy-farmer's daughter,
What milk I get I supplement with water.

[A huge Shadow is thrown on the road outside;
    LYDIA *starts.*

Whose shadow is it makes the highway darker?
That bullet head! .those ears! it is — Jack Parker!

[*Chord. The* CHORUS *flee in dismay, as* JACK
enters with a reckless swagger.

Song. — JACK PARKER.

I'm loafing about, and I very much doubt
If my excellent Ma is aware that I'm out;
My time I employ in attempts to annoy,
And I'm not what you'd call an agreeable boy!

> I shoe the cats with walnut-shells;
>   Tin cans to curs I tie;
> Ring furious knells at front-door bells —
>   Then round the corner fly!
> 'Neath donkeys' tails I fasten furze,
>   Or timid horsemen scare;
> If chance occurs, I stock with burrs
>   My little sister's hair!

>   [*The Bull shakes his head reprovingly.*

Such tricks give me joy without any alloy,
But they do not denote an agreeable boy!

[*As* JACK PARKER *concludes, the Bull ducks cau-
tiously below the half-door, while* LYDIA *conceals
herself behind the pump,* L. C.

JACK (*wandering about stage discontentedly*). I
  thought at least there'd be *some* beasts to
  badger here !
Call this a farm — there ain't a blooming spadger
  here !
  [*Approaches stall. Bull raises head suddenly.*
A bull ! This is a lark I've long awaited !
He's in a stable, so he should be baited !

[*The Bull shows symptoms of acute depression at this
  jeu de mots;* LYDIA *comes forward indignantly.*

LYDIA. I *can't* stand by and see that poor bull
  suffer !
Excitement's sure to make his beef taste tougher !
  [*The Bull emphatically corroborates this statement.*
Be warned by Miss Jane Taylor ; fractured skulls
Invariably come from teasing bulls !
So let that door alone, nor lift the latchet ;
For if the bull gets out — why, then you'll catch it !
JACK. A fractured skull ? Yah, don't believe a
  word of it !

[*Raises latchet: chord; Bull comes slowly out, and
  crouches ominously;* JACK *retreats, and takes
  refuge on top of pump; the Bull, after scratching
  his back with his off foreleg, makes a sudden rush
  at* LYDIA.

LYDIA (*as she evades it*). Here, help! — it's chasing me — it's too absurd of it!

Go away, Bull — with *me* you have no quarrel!

[*The Bull intimates that he is acting from a deep sense of duty.*

LYDIA (*impatiently*). You stupid thing, you're *ruining* the moral!

[*The Bull persists obstinately in his pursuit.*

JACK (*from top of pump*). Well dodged, Miss Banks! although the Bull I'll back!

[*Enter* FARM-HANDS.

LYDIA. Come quick — this Bull's mistaking me for Jack!

JACK. He knows his business best, I shouldn't wonder.

FARM-HANDS (*philosophically*). He ain't the sort of Bull to make a blunder.

[*They look on.*

LYDIA (*panting*). Such violent exercise will soon exhaust me!

[*The Bull comes behind her.*

Oh, Bull, it *is* unkind of you . . . you've *tossed* me!

[*Falls on ground, while the Bull stands over her, in readiness to give the coup de grace;* LYDIA *calls for help.*

A FARM-HAND (*encouragingly*). Nay, Miss, he
  seems moor sensible nor surly —
He knows as how good children perish early!

[*The Bull nods in acknowledgment that he is at last
  understood, and slaps his chest with his foreleys.*

LYDIA. Bull, I'll turn naughty, if you'll but be
  lenient!
Goodness, I see, is sometimes inconvenient.
I promise you henceforth I'll *try*, at any rate,
To act like children who are unregenerate!

[*The Bull, after turning this over, decides to accept
  a compromise.*

JACK. And, Lydia, when you ready for a lark
  are,
Just give a chyhike to your friend — Jack Parker!
                    [*They shake hands warmly.*

FINALE.

LYDIA. I thought to slowly fade away so calm
  and beautiful.
  (Though I didn't mean to go just yet) ;
But you get no chance for pathos when you're
  chivied by a bull!
  (Though I thought I wouldn't go just yet.)
For I did feel so upset, when I found that all you
  get

By the exercise of virtue, is that bulls will come
   and hurt you!
That I thought I wouldn't go just yet!

CHORUS.

We hear with some regret,
That she doesn't mean to go just yet.
But a Bull with horns that hurt you
Is a poor return for virtue,
So she's wiser not to go just yet!

[*The Bull rises on his hindlegs, and gives a forehoof
   each to* LYDIA *and* JACK, *who dance wildly round
   and round as the Curtain falls.*

[N. B. — Music-hall Managers are warned that
the morality of this particular Drama may possibly
be called in question by some members of the
L. C. C.

IX.—UNDER THE HARROW.

A CONVENTIONAL COMEDY-MELODRAMA, IN
TWO ACTS.

CHARACTERS.

SIR POSHBURY PUDDOCK (*a haughty and high-minded Baronet*).
VERBENA PUDDOCK (*his Daughter*).
LORD BLESHUGH (*her Lover*).
SPIKER (*a needy and unscrupulous adventurer*).
BLETHERS (*an ancient and attached Domestic*).

ACT I.

SCENE. — *The Morning Room at Natterjack Hall,
Toadley-le-Hole; large window open at back, with
heavy practicable sash.*

Enter BLETHERS.

BLETHERS. Sir Poshbury's birthday to-day —
his birthday! — and the gentry giving of him
presents. Oh, Lor! if they only knew what I
could tell 'em! . . . Ah! and *must* tell, too, before
long — but not yet — not yet!   [*Exit.*

177

Enter LORD BLESHUGH *and* VERBENA.

VERB. Yes, Papa is forty to-day (*innocently*); fancy living to *that* age ! The tenants have presented him with a handsome jar of mixed pickles, with an appropriate inscription. Papa is loved and respected by every one. And I — well, I have made him a little housewife, containing needles and thread. . . . See !   [*Shows it.*

LORD BLESH. (*tenderly*). I say, I — I wish you would make *me* a little housewife !

[*Comedy love-dialogue omitted owing to want of space.*

VERB. Oh, do look ! — there's papa crossing the lawn with, oh, such a horrid man following him !

LORD B. Regular bounder. Shocking bad hat !

VERB. Not so bad as his boots, and *they* are not so bad as his face ! Why doesn't Papa order him to go away? Oh, he is actually inviting him in !

Enter SIR POSHBURY, *gloomy and constrained, with* SPIKER, *who is jaunty and somewhat over familiar.*

SPIKER (*sitting on the piano, and dusting his boots with his handkerchief*). Cosey little shanty you've got here, Puddock — very tasty !

SIR P. (*with a gulp*). I am — ha — delighted that you approve of it! Ah, Verbena!

[*Kisses her on forehead.*

SPIKER. Your daughter, eh? Pooty gal. Introduce me.

[SIR POSH. *introduces him — with an effort.*

VERB. (*coldly*). How do you do? Papa, did you know that the sash-line of this window was broken? If it is not mended, it will fall on somebody's head, and perhaps kill him!

SIR P. (*absently*). Yes — yes, it shall be attended to; but leave us, my child, go. Bleshugh, this — er — gentleman and I have business of importance to discuss.

SPIKER. Don't let us drive you away, Miss; your Pa and me are only talking over old times, that's all — eh, Posh?

SIR P. (*in a tortured aside*). Have a care, sir, don't drive me too far! (*To* VERB.). Leave us, I say. (LORD B. *and* VERB. *go out, raising their eyebrows.*) Now, sir, what is this secret you profess to have discovered?

SPIKER. Oh, a mere nothing. (*Takes out a cigar.*) Got a light about you? Thanks. Perhaps you don't recollect twenty-seven years ago this very day, travelling from Edgware Road to Baker Street, by the Underground Railway?

SIR P. Perfectly; it was my thirteenth birth-day, and I celebrated the event by a visit to Madame Tussaud's.

SPIKER. Exactly; it was your thirteenth birth-day, and you travelled second-class with a half-ticket — (*meaningly*) — on your thirteenth birth-day.

SIR P. (*terribly agitated*). Fiend that you are, how came you to learn this?

SPIKER. Very simple. I was at that time in the temporary position of ticket-collector at Baker Street. In the exuberance of boyhood, you cheeked me. I swore to be even with you some day.

SIR P. Even if — if your accusation were well-founded, how are you going to prove it?

SP. Oh, that's easy! I preserved the half-ticket, on the chance that I should require it as evidence hereafter.

SIR P. (*aside*). And so the one error of an otherwise blameless boyhood has found me out — at last! (*To* SPIKER.) I fear you not; my crime — if crime indeed it was — is surely con-doned by twenty-seven long years of unimpeach-able integrity!

SP. By-laws are By-laws, old Buck! there's no Statute of Limitations in criminal offences that ever *I* heard of! Nothing can alter the fact that you, being turned thirteen, obtained a half-ticket by a false representation that you were under age. A line from me, even now, denouncing you to the Traffic Superintendent, and I'm very much afraid—

SIR P. (*writhing*). Spiker, my — my dear friend, you won't do that, you won't expose me? Think of my age, my position, my daughter!

SP. Ah, now you've touched the right chord! I *was* thinking of your daughter — a nice lady-like gal — I don't mind telling you she fetched me, sir, at the first glance. Give me her hand, and I burn the compromising half-ticket before your eyes on our return from church after the wedding. Come, that's a fair offer!

SIR P. (*indignantly*). My child, the ripening apple of my failing eye, to be sacrificed to a black-mailing blackguard like you! Never while I live!

SP. Just as you please; and, if you will kindly oblige me with writing materials, I will just drop a line to the Traffic Superintendent—

SIR P. (*hoarsely*). No, no, not *that*. . . . Wait, listen; I — I will speak to my daughter. I promise nothing; but if her heart is still her own to

give, she may (mind, I do say she *will*), be induced to link her lot to yours, though I shall not
attempt to influence her in any way — in *any* way.

SP.   Well, you know your own business best,
old Cockalorum.   Here comes the young lady, so
I'll leave you to manage this delicate affair alone.
Ta-ta.   I sha'n't be far off.

[*Swaggers insolently out as* VERB. *enters.*

SIR P.   My child, I have just received an offer
for your hand.   I know not if you will consent?

VERB.   I can guess who has made that offer,
and why.   I consent with all my heart, dear Papa.

SIR P.   Can I trust my ears!   You consent?
Noble girl!   [*He embraces her.*

VERB.   I was quite sure dear Bleshugh meant
to speak, and I *do* love him very much.

SIR P. (*starting*).   It is not Lord Bleshugh, my
child, but Mr. Samuel Spiker, the gentleman (for
he is at heart a gentleman) whom I introduced to
you just now.

VERB.   I have seen so little of him, Papa, I
cannot love him — you must really excuse me!

SIR P.   Ah, but you will, my darling, you *will*
— I know your unselfish nature — you will, to save
your poor old dad from a terrible disgrace . . . yes,
disgrace, listen!   Twenty-seven years ago — (*he*

tells her all). Verbena, at this very moment, there is a subscription on foot in the county to present me with my photograph, done by an itinerant photographer of the highest eminence, and framed and glazed ready for hanging. Is that photograph never to know the nail which even now awaits it? Can you not surrender a passing girlish fancy, to spare your fond old father's fame? Mr. Spiker is peculiar, perhaps, in many ways — not quite of our *monde* — but he loves you, sincerely, my child, and that is in itself a recommendation. Ah, I see — my prayers are vain . . . be happy, then. As for me, let the police come — I am ready! [*Weeps.*

VERB. Not so, Papa; I will marry this Mr. Spiker, since it is your wish.

[SIR POSH. *dries his eyes.*

SIR P. Here, Spiker, my dear fellow, it is all right. Come in. She accepts you.

Enter SPIKER.

SP. Thought she would. Sensible little gal! Well, Miss, you sha'n't regret it. Bless you, we'll be as chummy together as a couple of little dicky-birds.

VERB. Mr. Spiker, let us understand one another. I will do my best to be a good wife to you

— but chumminess is not mine to give, nor can I promise ever to be your dicky-bird.

Enter LORD BLESHUGH.

LORD B. Sir Poshbury, may I have five minutes with you? Verbena, you need not go. (*Looking at* SPIKER.) Perhaps this person will kindly relieve us of his presence.

SP. Sorry to disoblige, old fellow, but I'm on duty where Miss Verbena is now, you see, as she's just promised to be my wife.

LORD B. *Your* wife!

VERB. (*faintly*). Yes, Lord Bleshugh, his *wife!*

SIR P. Yes, my poor boy, *his* wife!

[VERBENA *totters, and falls heavily in a dead faint,* R. C., *upsetting a flower-stand;* LORD BLESHUGH *staggers, and swoons on sofa,* C., *overturning a table of knickknacks;* SIR POSHBURY *sinks into chair,* L. C., *and covers his face with his hands.*

SP. (*looking down on them triumphantly*). Under the Harrow, by Gad! Under the Harrow!

[*Curtain, and end of Act I.*

ACT II.

SCENE. — *Same as in Act I.; viz., the Morning-Room at Natterjack Hall. Evening of same day. Enter* BLETHERS.

BLETHERS. Another of Sir Poshbury's birth-days almost gone — and my secret still untold! (*Dodders.*) I can't keep it up much longer. . . . Ha, here comes his Lordship — he does look mortal bad, that he do! Miss Verbena ain't treated him too well, from all I can hear, poor young feller!

Enter LORD BLESHUGH.

LORD BLESHUGH. Blethers, by the memory of the innumerable half-crowns that have passed be-tween us, be my friend now — I have no others left. Persuade your young Mistress to come hither — you need not tell her *I* am here, you understand. Be discreet, and this florin shall be yours!

BLETHERS. Leave it to me, my lord. I'd tell a lie for less than that, any day, old as I am!

[*Exit.*

LORD BL. I cannot rest till I have heard from her own lips that the past few hours have been nothing but a horrible dream. . . . She is coming! Now for the truth!

Enter VERBENA.

VERBENA.   Papa, did you want me?   (*Recognizes* LORD B. — *controls herself to a cold formality.*) My lord, to what do I owe this — this unexpected intrusion?   [*Pants violently.*

LORD BL.   Verbena, tell me, you cannot really prefer that seedy snob in the burst boots to me?

VERB.   (*aside*).   How can I tell him the truth without betraying dear Papa?   No, I must lie, though it kills me.   (*To* LORD B.)   Lord Bleshugh, I have been trifling with you.   I — I never loved you.

LORD B.   I see, and all the while your heart was given to a howling cad?

VERB.   And if it was, who can account for the vagaries of a girlish fancy!   We women are capricious beings, you know.   (*With hysterical gayety.*) But you are unjust to Mr. Spiker — he has not *yet* howled in *my* presence — (*aside*) — though I very nearly did in *his!*

LORD B.   And you really love him?

VERB.   I — I love him.   (*Aside.*)   My heart will break!

LORD B.   Then I have no more to say.   Farewell, Verbena!   Be as happy as the knowledge that you have wrecked one of the brightest careers, and soured one of the sweetest natures in the county, will permit. (*Goes up stage, and returns.*) A few days since you presented me with a cloth pen-wiper, in the shape of a dog of unknown breed. If you will kindly wait here for half-an-hour, I shall have much pleasure in returning a memento which I have no longer the right to retain, and there are several little things I gave you which I can take back with me at the same time, if you will have them put up in readiness.   [*Exit.*

VERB. Oh, he is cruel, cruel! but I shall keep the little bone yard-measure, and the diamond pig — they are all I have to remind me of him!

Enter SPIKER, *slightly intoxicated.*

SPIKER (*throwing himself on sofa without seeing* VERB.) I don' know how it is, but I feel precioush shleepy, somehow. P'raps I *did* partake lil' too freely of Sir Poshbury's gen'rous Burgundy. Wunner why they call it "gen'rous" — it didn't give *me* anything — 'cept a bloomin' headache! However, I punished it, and old Poshbury had to look on and let me. He-he! (*Examining his hand.*) Who'd think, to look at thish thumb, that there was a real live Baronet squirmin' under it. But there ish!   [*Snores.*

VERB. (*bitterly*).   And *that* thing is my affianced husband!   Ah, no, I cannot go through with it; he is *too* repulsive!   If I could but find a way to free myself without compromising poor Papa.   The sofa-cushion!   *Dare* I?   It would be quite pain- less. . . .   Surely the removal of such an odious wretch cannot be *Murder*. . . . I will!   (*Slow music.   She gets a cushion, and presses it tightly over* SPIKER's *head.*)   Oh, I *wish* he wouldn't gurgle like that, and how he does kick!   He can- not even die like a gentleman!   (SPIKER's *kicks become more and more feeble, and eventually cease.*)   How still he lies!   I almost wish. . . . Mr. Spiker, Mr. Spi-ker! . . . no answer — oh, I really *have* suffocated him!   (*Enter* SIR POSH.)   You, Papa?

SIR POSH.   What, Verbena, sitting with, hem — Samuel in the gloaming?   (*Sings with forced hilarity.*)   " In the gloaming, oh, my darling! " that's as it should be — quite as it should be!

VERB. (*in dull, strained accents*).   Don't sing, Papa, I cannot bear it — just yet.   I have just suffocated Mr. Spiker with a sofa-cushion.   See!

[*Shows the body.*

SIR P.   Then I am safe — he will tell no tales now!   But, my child, are you aware of the very serious nature of your act? An act of which, as a Justice of the Peace, I am bound to take some official cognizance!

VERB. Do not scold me, Papa. Was it not done for *your* sake?

SIR P. I cannot accept such an excuse as that. I fear your motives were less disinterested than you would have me believe. And now, Verbena, what will *you* do? As your father, I would gladly screen you — but, as a Magistrate, I cannot promise to be more than passive.

VERB. Listen, Papa. I have thought of a plan. Why should I not wheel this sofa to the head of the front-door steps, and tip it over? They will only think he fell down when intoxicated — for he *had* taken far too much wine, Papa!

SIR P. Always the same quick-witted little fairy! Go, my child, but be careful that none of the servants see you. (VERB. *wheels the sofa and* SPIKER'S *body out*, L. U. E.) My poor impulsive darling, I do hope she will not be seen — servants *do* make such mischief! But there's an end of Spiker, at any rate. I should *not* have liked him for a son-in-law, and with him goes the only person who knows my unhappy secret!

Enter BLETHERS.

BLETHERS. Sir Poshbury, I have a secret to reveal which I can preserve no longer — it concerns something that happened many years ago — it is connected with your *birthday*, Sir Poshbury.

SIR P. (*quailing*). What, *another!* I must stop *his* tongue at all hazards. Ah, the rotten sash-line! (*To* BLETHERS.) I will hear you, but first close yonder window, the night-air is growing chill.

[BLETHERS *goes to window at back. Slow music. As he approaches it* LORD BLESHUGH *enters* (R 2 E), *and, with a smothered cry of horror, drags him back by the coat-tails — just before the window falls with a tremendous crash.*

SIR P. Bleshugh! What have you done?

LORD BLESH. (*sternly*). Saved *him* from an untimely end — and *you* from — crime.

Collapse of SIR P. *Enter* VERBENA, *terrified.*

VERB. Papa, Papa, hide me! The night air and the cold stone steps have restored Mr. Spiker to life and consciousness! He is coming to denounce me — you — both of us! He is awfully annoyed!

SIR P. (*recklessly*). It is useless to appeal to me, child. I have enough to do to look after myself — now.

[*Enter* SPIKER, *indignant.*

SPIKER. Pretty treatment for a gentleman, this! Look here, Poshbury, this young lady has choked me with a cushion, and then pitched me down the front steps — I might have broken my neck.

SIR P. It was an oversight which I lament, but for which I must decline to be answerable. You must settle your differences with her.

SPIKER. And you too, old horse! *You* had a hand in this, I know, and I'll pay you out for it now. My life ain't safe if I marry a girl like that, so I've made up my mind to split and be done with it!

SIR P. (*contemptuously*). If *you* don't, Blethers *will.* So do your worst, you hound!

SPIKER. Very well then; I will. (*To the rest.*) I denounce this man for travelling with a half-ticket from Edgware Road to Baker Street on his thirteenth birthday, the 31st of March, twenty-seven years ago this very day! [*Sensation.*

BLETHERS. Hear me! It was *not* his thirteenth birthday; Sir Poshbury's birthday falls on the 1st of April — *to-morrow!* I was sent to register the birth, and, by a blunder, which I have repented bitterly ever since, unfortunately gave the wrong date. Till this moment I have never had the manliness or sincerity to confess my error, for fear of losing my situation.

SIR P. (*to* SPIKER). Do you hear, you paltry knave? I was *not* thirteen. Consequently I was under age, and the By-laws are still unbroken. Your hold over me is gone — gone forever!

SPIKER. H'm — Spiker spiked this time!

[*Retires up disconcerted.*

LORD B. And you did not really love him after all, Verbena?

VERB. (*with arch pride*). Have I not proved my indifference?

LORD B. But I forget — you admitted that you were but trifling with my affection — take back your pin-cushion!

VERB. Keep it. All that I did was done to spare my father!

SIR POSH. Who, as a matter of fact, was innocent — but I forgive you, child, for your unworthy suspicions. Bleshugh, my boy, you have saved me from unnecessarily depriving myself of the services of an old retainer. Blethers, I condone a dissimulation for which you have done much to atone. Spiker, you vile and miserable rascal, be off, and be thankful that I have sufficient magnanimity to refrain from giving you in charge. (SPIKER *sneaks off crushed.*) And now, my children, and my faithful old servant, congratulate me that I am no longer —

VERBENA *and* LORD BLESHUGH (*together*). Under the Harrow.

[*Affecting Family Tableau and quick Curtain.*

X. — TOMMY AND HIS SISTER JANE.

ONCE more we draw upon our favorite source of inspiration, — the poems of the Misses Taylor. The dramatist is serenely confident that the new London County Council Censor of Plays, whenever that much-desired official is appointed, will highly approve of this little piece, on account of the multiplicity of its morals. It is intended to teach, amongst other useful lessons, that — as the poem on which it is founded puts it — "Fruit in lanes is seldom good;" also, that it is not always prudent to take a hint: again, that constructive murder is distinctly reprehensible, and should never be indulged in by persons who cannot control their countenances afterwards. Lastly, that suicide may often be averted by the exercise of a little *savoir vivre*.

TOMMY AND HIS SISTER JANE.

CHARACTERS.

TOMMY AND HIS SISTER JANE (*Taylorian Twins, and awful examples*).

THEIR WICKED UNCLE (*plagiarized from a forgotten Nursery Story, and slightly altered*).

OLD FARMER COPEER (*skilled in the use of horse and cattle medicines*).

SCENE. — *A shady lane; on the right, a gate lead-ing to the farm; left, some bushes, covered with practicable scarlet berries.*

Enter the WICKED UNCLE, *stealthily.*

THE W. U.   No peace of mind I e'er shall know
    again

Till I have cooked the geese of Tom and Jane!

But — though a naughty — I'm a nervous nunky,

For downright felonies I'm far too funky!

I'd hire assassins — but of late the villains

Have raised their usual fee to fifteen shillin's!

Nor, to reduce their rates, will they engage

(*Sympathetically.*)   For two orphans who are
    under age!

So (as I'd give no more than half a guinea)

I must myself get rid of Tom and Jenny.

Yet, like an old soft-hearted fool, I falter,

And can't make up my mind to risk a halter.

(*Looking off.*)   Ha, in the distance, Jane and
    little Tom I see!

These berries (*meditatively*) — why it only needs
    diplomacy.

Ho-ho, a most ingenious experiment!

[*Indulges in silent and sinister mirth, as* JANE *and*
    TOM *trip in, and regard him with innocent
    wonder.*

JANE. Uncle, what *is* the joke? Why all this
    merriment?

THE W. U. (*in guilty confusion*). Not merriment,
    my loves — a trifling spasm —

Don't be alarmed — your uncle often has 'em!

I'm feeling better than I did at first —

You're looking flushed, though not, I hope with
    thirst?

                             [*Insidiously.*

        Song by the WICKED UNCLE.

  The sun is scorching overhead;

    The roads are dry and dusty;

  And here are berries ripe and red,

    Refreshing when you're *thusty!*

  They're hanging just within your reach,

    Inviting you to clutch them!

  But — as your Uncle — I beseech

    You won't attempt to touch them?

TOMMY *and* JANE (*dutifully*). We'll do whatever
    you beseech, and not attempt to touch them!

                   [*Annoyance of* W. U.

THE W. U.

  Temptation (so I've understood)

    A child, in order kept, shuns;

  And fruit in lanes is seldom good

    (With several exceptions).

However freely you partake,
 It can't — as you are young — kill,
But should it cause a stomach-ache —
 Well, don't blame your Uncle!

TOMMY *and* JANE. No, should it cause a stomach-ache, we will not blame our Uncle!

THE W. U. (*aside*). They'll need no further personal assistance,
But take the bait when I am at a distance.
I could not, were I paid a thousand ducats,
(*With sentiment.*) Stand by, and see them kick their little buckets,
Or look on while their sticks this pretty pair cut!
        [*Stealing off.*

TOMMY. What, Uncle, going?

THE W. U. (*with assumed jauntiness*). Just to get my hair cut!   [*Goes.*

TOMMY (*looking wistfully at the berries*). I say, they *do* look nice, Jane, such a lot too!

JANE (*demurely*). Well, Tommy, Uncle never told us *not* to.

[*Slow music; they gradually approach the berries, which they pick and eat with increasing relish, culminating in a dance of delight.*

Duet. — TOMMY *and* JANE (*with step-dance*).

TOMMY (*dancing, with his mouth full*). These
   berries ain't so bad — although they've far
   too much acidity.

JANE (*ditto*). To me, their only drawback is a
   dash of insipidity.

TOMMY (*rudely*). But, all the same, you're
   wolfing 'em with wonderful avidity !

JANE (*indignantly*). No, *that* I'm not, so *there*
   now !

TOMMY (*calmly*).   But you *are!*

JANE.   And so are *you!*

[*They retire up, dancing, and eat more berries —
   after which they gaze thoughtfully at each other.*

JANE. This fruit is most refreshing — but it's
   curious how it cloys on you !.

TOMMY (*with anxiety*). I wonder why all appetite
   for dinner it destroys in you !

JANE. Oh, Tommy, aren't you half afraid you've
   ate enough to poison you ?

TOMMY. No, *that* I'm not — so there now ! etc.

                [*They dance as before.*

TOMMY. Jane, *is* your palate parching up in horrible aridity ?

JANE. It is, and in my throat's a lump of singular
   solidity.

Tommy. Then that is why you're dancing with such poker-like rigidity.

[*Refrain as before; they dance with decreasing spirit, and finally stop, and fan one another with their hats.*

Jane. I'm better now that on my brow there is a little breeziness.

Tommy. My passing qualm is growing calm, and tightness turns to easiness.

Jane. You seem to me tormented by a tendency to queasiness?

[*Refrain; they attempt to continue the dance — but suddenly sit down side by side.*

Jane (*with a gasp*). I don't know what it is — but, oh, I *do* feel so peculiar!

Tommy (*with a gulp*). I've tumults taking place within that I may say unruly are.

Jane. Why, Tommy, you are turning green — you really and you *truly* are!

Tommy. No, *that* I'm not, so *there* now!

Jane.   But you *are!*

Tommy.   And so are *you!*

[*Melancholy music; to which* Tommy *and* Jane, *after a few convulsive movements, gradually become inanimate. Enter old* Farmer Copeer *from gate, carrying a large bottle labelled " Cattle Medicine."*

FARMER C.   It's time I gave the old bay mare her
    drench.   *[Stumbles over the children.*
What's here?   A lifeless lad! — and little wench!
Been eating berries — where did they get *them*
    idees?

For cows, when took so, I've the reg'lar remedies.
I'll try 'em here — and if their state the worse is,
Why, they shall have them balls I give my 'erses!

[Carries the bodies off just before the W. U. *re-enters.*

W. U.   The children — gone? yon bush of ber-
    ries less full!

Hooray, my little stratagem's successful!

[Dances a triumphant pas seul. Re-enter FARMER C.

FARMER C.   Been looking for your little niece
    and nephew?

THE W. U.   Yes, searching for them every-
    where —

FARMER C. (*ironically*).   Oh, *hev* you?
Then let me tell you, from all pain they're free, sir.

THE W. U. (*falling on his knees*).   *I* didn't poison
    them — it wasn't *me*, sir!

FARMER C.   I thought as much — a constable I'll
    run for.   *[Exit.*

THE W. U.   My wretched nerves again! *This*
    time I'm done for!

Well, though I'm trapped, and useless all disguise is,
My case shall ne'er come on at the Assizes!

[*Rushes desperately to tree and crams himself with the remaining berries, which produce an almost instantaneous effect. Re-enter* TOM *and* JANE *from gate, looking pale and limp. Terror of the* WICKED UNCLE *as he turns and recognizes them.*

THE W. U. (*with tremulous politeness*). The shades of Jane and Tommy, I presume?

[*Re-enter* FARMER C.

JANE AND TOMMY (*pointing to* FARMER C.). His Cattle Mixtures snatched us from the tomb!

THE W. U. (*with a flicker of hope*). Why, then the self-same drugs will ease *my* torments!

FARMER C. (*chuckling*). Too late! they've drunk the lot, the little vormints!

THE W. U. (*bitterly*). So out of life I must inglorious wriggle,
Pursued by Tommy's grin, and Jenny's giggle!

[*Dies in great agony, while* TOMMY, JANE, *and* FARMER COPEER *look on with mixed emotions as the Curtain falls.*

XI.—THE RIVAL DOLLS.

"Miss Jenny and Polly had each a new dolly."—*Vide Poem.*

CHARACTERS.

MISS JENNY . . . . } By the Sisters LEAMAR.
MISS POLLY . . . . }

THE SOLDIER DOLL . } By the Two ARMSTRONGS.
THE SAILOR DOLL . }

SCENE.—*A Nursery. Enter* MISS JENNY *and*
MISS POLLY, *who perform a blameless step-dance
with an improving chorus.*

Oh, isn't it jolly! we've each a new dolly,
   And one is a Soldier, the other's a Tar;
We're fully contented with what's been presented,
   Such good little children we both of us are!

[*They dance up to a cupboard, from which they bring
out two large Dolls, which they place on chairs.*

MISS J. *Don't* they look nice! Come, Polly, let
   us strive
To make ourselves believe that they're alive!
MISS P. (*addressing* SAILOR D.). I'm glad you're
   mine. I dote on all that's nautical.

THE SAILOR D. (*opening his eyes suddenly*). Excuse me, Miss, your sister's more *my* sort o' gal.

[*Kisses his hand to* MISS J., *who shrinks back, shocked and alarmed.*

MISS J.   Oh, Polly, *did* you hear?   I feel so shy!

THE SAILOR D. (*with mild self-assertion*). *I* can say "Pa" and "Ma" — and wink my eye.

[*Does so at* MISS P., *who runs in terror to* MISS J.'s *side.*

MISS J.   Why, both are showing signs of animation!

MISS P.   Who'd think we had such strong imagination!

THE SOLDIER D. (*aside to the* SAILOR D.).   I say, old fellow, we have caught their fancy —

In each of us they now a real man see!

Let's keep it up!

THE SAILOR D. (*dubiously*).   D'ye think as we can *do* it?

THE SOLDIER D.   You stick by me, and I will see you through it.

Sit up, and turn your toes out, — don't you loll;

Put on the Man, and drop the bloomin' Doll!

[*The* SAILOR DOLL *pulls himself together, and rises from chair importantly.*

THE SAILOR D. (*in the manner of a Music-hall Chairman*).   Ladies, with your kind leave, this gallant gent

Will now his military sketch present.

[MISS J. *and* P. *applaud: the* SOLDIER D., *after feebly expostulating, is induced to sing.*

Song, by the SOLDIER DOLL.

When I used to be displayed,
In the Burlington Arcade,
With artillery arrayed
    Underneath.
        Shoulder Hump!

I imagine that I made
All the Lady Dolls afraid,
I should draw my battle-blade
    From its sheath,
        Shoulder Hump!

For I'm Mars's gallant son,
And my back I've shown to none,
Nor was ever seen to run
    From the strife !
        Shoulder Hump!

Oh, the battles I'd have won,
And the dashing deeds have done,
If I'd ever fired a gun
In my life !
Shoulder Hump !

Refrain (to be sung marching round Stage).
By your right flank, Wheel !
Let the front rank kneel !
With the bristle of the steel
To the foe.
Till their regiments reel,
At our rattling peal,
And the military zeal
We show !

[*Repeat, with the whole company marching round after him.*

THE SOLDIER D. My friend will next oblige — this jolly Jack Tar.
Will give his song and chorus in charàck-tar !

[*Same business with* SAILOR D.

Song, by the SAILOR DOLL.
In costume I'm
So maritime,
You'd never suppose the fact is,

That with the Fleet
In Regent Street,   .
I'd precious little naval practice!
There was saucy craft,
Rigged fore an' aft,
Inside o' Mr. Cre-mer's.
From Noah's Arks to Clipper-built barks,
Like-wise mechanical stea-mers.

Chorus.

But to navigate the Serpentine,
    Yeo-ho, my lads, ahoy!
With clockwork, sails, or spirits of wine,
    Yeo-ho, my lads, ahoy!
I did respeckfully decline,
So I was left in port to pine,
Which wasn't azactually the line
Of a rollicking Sailor Boy, Yeo-ho!
Of a rollicking Sailor Bo-oy!

Yes, there was lots
Of boats and yachts,
Of timber and of tin, too;
But one and all
Was far too small
For a doll o' my size to get into.

I was too big
On any brig
To ship without disas-ter,
And it wouldn't never do
When the cap'n and the crew
Were a set o' little swabs all plaster!

Chorus.

So to navigate the Serpentine, etc.

An Ark is p'raps
The berth for chaps
As is fond o' Natural Hist'ry.
But I sez to Shem
And the rest o' them,
" How you get along at all's a myst'ry!
With a Wild Beast Show
Let loose below,
And four fe-males on deck too !
I never could agree
With your happy fami-lee,
And your lubberly ways I objeck to."

[*Chorus.   Hornpipe by the company, after which
the* SOLDIER DOLL *advances condescendingly to*
MISS JENNY.

The Soldier D.   Invincible I'm reckoned by the
   Ladies,
But yield to you — though conquering my trade
   is !
Miss J. (*repulsing him*).   Oh, go away, you great
   conceited thing, you !

[*The* Soldier *persists in offering her attentions.*

Miss P. (*watching them bitterly*).   To be deserted
   by one's doll *does* sting you !

[*The* Sailor D. *approaches.*

The Sailor D. (*to* Miss P.)   Let *me* console you,
   Miss, a Sailor Doll
As swears his 'art was ever true to Poll !

(*N. B.*— *Good opportunity for Song here.*)

Miss P. (*indignantly to* Miss J.).   Your Sailor's
   teasing me to be his idol !
Do make him stop — (*spitefully*) — when you've
   quite done with *my* doll !.
Miss J. (*scornfully*).   If you suppose *I* want your
   wretched warrior,
I'm sorry *for* you !
Miss P.   I for you am sorrier.
Miss J. (*weeping*, R.).   Polly preferred to me —
   what ignominy !

Miss P. (*weeping*, L.).   My horrid Soldier jilting
    me for Jenny!

       [*The two dolls face one another,* C.

Sailor D. (*to* Soldier D.).   You've made her
    sluice her skylights now, you swab!

Soldier D. (*to* Sailor D.).   As you have broke
    her heart, I'll break your nob!   [*Hits him.*

Sailor D. (*in a pale fury*).   This insult must be
    blotted out in bran!

Soldier D. (*fiercely*).   Come on, I'll shed your
    sawdust — if I can!

[Miss J. *and* P. *throw themselves between the com-
batants.*

Miss J.   For any mess you make *we* shall be
    scolded,

So wait until a drugget we've unfolded!

       [*They lay down drugget on Stage.*

The Soldier D. (*politely*).   No hurry, Miss, *we*
    don't object to waiting.

The Sailor D. (*aside*).   His valor — like my
    own —'s evaporating!

(*Defiantly to* Soldier D.).   On guard!   You'll
    see how soon I'll run you through!

(*Confidentially.*)   (If you will not prod *me*, I
    won't pink *you*.)

THE SOLDIER D. Through your false kid my
    deadly blade I'll pass!

(*Confidentially*). (Look here, old fellow, don't
    you be *a hass!*)

    [*They exchange passes at a considerable distance.*

THE SAILOR D. (*aside*). Don't lose your temper
    now!

SOLDIER D.   Don't get excited.

Do keep a little farther off!

SAILOR D.   Delighted!

    [*Wounds* SOLDIER D., *by misadventure.*

SOLDIER D. (*annoyed*). There now, you've gone
    and made upon my wax a dent!

SAILOR D. Excuse me, it was really quite an
    accident.

SOLDIER D. (*savagely*). Such clumsiness would
    irritate a saint!   [*Stabs* SAILOR DOLL.

MISS J. *and* P. (*imploringly*). Oh, stop! the sight
    of sawdust turns us faint!

    [*They drop into chairs, swooning.*

SAILOR D. I'll pay you out for that!

    [*Stabs* SOLDIER D.

SOLDIER. D.   Right through you've poked me!

SAILOR D. So you have *me!*

SOLDIER D.   You shouldn't have provoked me!

    [*They fall transfixed.*

SAILOR D. (*faintly*). Alas, we have been led
    away by vanity.

Dolls shouldn't try to imitate humanity!   [*Dies.*

SOLDIER D. For, if they do, they'll end like us,
    unpitied,

Each on the other's sword absurdly spitted!

[*Dies.* MISS J. *and* P. *revive, and bend sadly over
the corpses.*

MISS JENNY. From their untimely end we draw
    this moral,

How wrong it is, even for dolls, to quarrel!

MISS POLLY. Yes, Jenny, in the fate of these
    poor fellows see

What sad results may spring from female jealousy!

[*They embrace penitently as Curtain falls.*

XII. — CONRAD; OR THE THUMB-SUCKER.

(ADAPTED FREELY FROM A WELL-KNOWN POEM IN THE "STRUWWELPETER.")

CHARACTERS.

CONRAD (*aged 6*).
CONRAD'S MOTHER (47).
THE SCISSORMAN (*age immaterial*).

SCENE. — *An apartment in the house of* CONRAD'S
MOTHER, *window in centre at back, opening upon
a quiet thoroughfare. It is dusk, and the room is
lighted only by the reflected gleam from the street-
lamps.* CONRAD *discovered half-hidden by left
window-curtain.*

CONRAD (*watching street*). Still there! For
    full an hour he has not budged
Beyond the circle of yon lamp-post's rays!
The gaslight falls upon his crimson hose,
And makes a steely glitter at his thigh,
While from the shadow peers a hatchet-face
And fixes sinister malignant eyes —

On whom ? (*Shuddering.*)   I dare not trust my-
    self to guess
And yet — ah, no — it cannot be myself !
I am so young — one is still young at six ! —
What man can say that I have injured him?
Since, in my mother's absence all the day
Engaged upon Municipal affairs,
I peacefully beguile the weary hours
By suction of consolatory thumbs.

[*Here he inserts his thumb in his mouth, but almost
    instantly removes it with a start.*

Again I meet those eyes !   I'll look no more —
But draw the blind and shut my terror out.

      [*Draws blind and lights candle ; Stage lightens.*

Heigho, I wish my Mother were at home !
(*Listening.*)   At last !   I hear her latch-key in the
    door !

[*Enter* CONRAD'S MOTHER, *a lady of strong-minded
appearance, rationally attired.   She carries a
large reticule full of documents.*

    CONRAD'S M.   Would, Conrad, that you were
      of riper years,
So you might share your Mother's joy to-day,
The day that crowns her long and arduous toil
As one of London's County Councillors !

CONRAD. Nay, speak; for though my mind be
    immature,
One topic still can charm my infant ear,
That ever craves the oft-repeated tale.
I love to hear of that august assembly
       [*His* MOTHER *lifts her bonnet solemnly.*
In which my Mother's honored voice is raised!
    C.'s M. (*gratified*). Learn, Conrad, then, that,
    after many months
Of patient "lobbying" (you've heard the term?)
The measure by my foresight introduced
Has triumphed by a bare majority !
    CON. My bosom thrills with dutiful delight —
Although I yet for information wait
As to the scope and purpose of the statute.
    C.'s M. You show an interest so intelligent
That well deserves it should be satisfied.
Be seated, Conrad, at your Mother's knee,
And you shall hear the full particulars.
You know how zealously I advocate
The sacred cause of Nursery Reform?
How through my efforts every infant's toys
Are carefully inspected once a month ? —
    CON. (*wearily*). Nay, Mother, you forget — I
    have no toys.
    C.'s M. Which brings you under the exemption
    clause.

But — to resume; how Nursery Songs and Tales
Must now be duly licensed by our Censor,
And any deviation from the text
Forbidden under heavy penalties?
All that you know. Well; with concern of late,
I have remarked among our infancy
The rapid increase of a baneful habit
On which I scarce can bring my tongue to dwell.

[The Stage darker; blind at back illuminated.
Oh, Conrad, there are children — think of it! —
So lost to every sense of decency
That, in mere wantonness or brainless sloth,
They obstinately suck forbidden thumbs!

*[*CONRAD *starts with irrepressible emotion.*
Forgive me if I shock your innocence!
(*Sadly.*) Such things exist — but soon shall cease
          to be,
Thanks to the measure we have passed to-day!

  CON. (*with growing uneasiness*). But how can
    statutes check such practices?

  C.'s M. (*patting his head*). Right shrewdly
    questioned, boy! I come to that.

Some timid sentimentalist advised
Compulsory restraint in woollen gloves,
Or the deterrent aid of bitter aloes.
I saw the evil had too deep a seat

To yield to such half-hearted remedies.
No; we must cut, ere we could hope to cure!
Nay, interrupt me not; my Bill appoints
A new official, by the style and title
Of "London County Council Scissorman,"
For the detection of young "suck-a-thumbs."

[*Here the shadow of a huge hand brandishing a
    gigantic pair of shears appears upon the blind.*

    CON. (*hiding his face in his* MOTHER'S *lap.*)   Ah,
        Mother, see! . . . the scissors! . . . On the
        blind!

    C.'s M.   Why, how you tremble!   You've no
        cause to fear.

The shadow of his grim insignia
Should have no terror — save for thumbsuckers.

    CON.   And what for *them?*

    C.'s M. (*complacently*).   A doom devised by me —

The confiscation of the culprit's thumbs.
Thus shall our statute cure while it corrects,
For those who have no thumbs can err no more.

[*The shadow slowly passes on the blind,* CONRAD
    *appearing relieved at its departure.   Loud knock-
    ing without.   Both start to their feet.*

    C.'s M.   Who knocks so loud at such an hour
        as this?

A Voice.   Open, I charge ye.   In the Council's
    name!

C.'s M.   'Tis the Official Red-legged Scissorman,
Who doubtless calls to thank me for the post.

Con. (*with a gloomy determination*).   More like
    his business, Madam, is with — Me!

C.'s M. (*suddenly enlightened*).   A Suck-a-thumb?
    . . . *you*, Conrad?

Con. (*desperately*).   Ay, — from birth!

[*Profound silence, as Mother and Son face one another.   The knocking is renewed.*

C.'s M.   Oh, this is horrible — it must not be!
I'll shoot the bolt and barricade the door.

[Conrad *places himself before it, and addresses his
Mother in a tone of incisive irony.*

Con.   Why, where is all the zeal you showed
    of late?
Is't thus that you the Roman Matron play?
Trick not a statute of your own devising.
Come, your official's waiting — let him in!

            [C.'s M. *shrinks back appalled.*

So? you refuse! — (*throwing open door*) — then —
    enter, Scissorman!

[*Enter the* Scissorman, *masked and in red tights,
with his hand upon the hilt of his shears.*

THE S. (*in a passionless tone*).   Though sorry
to create unpleasantness,
I claim the thumbs of this young gentleman,
Which these own eyes have marked between his
lips.
C.'s M. (*frantically*).   Thou minion of a meddling
tyranny,
Go exercise thy loathsome trade elsewhere!
THE S. (*civilly*).   I've duties here that must be
first performed.
C.'s M. (*wildly*).   Take my two thumbs for his!
THE S.   'Tis not the law —
Which is a model of lucidity.
CON. (*calmly*).   Sir, you speak well. My thumbs
are forfeited,
And they alone must pay the penalty.
THE S. (*with approval*).   Right! Step with me
into the outer hall,
And have the business done without delay.
C.'s M. (*throwing herself between them.*)   Stay,
I'm a Councillor — this law was *mine!*
Hereby I do suspend the clause I drew.
THE S.   You should have drawn it milder.
CON..   Must I teach
A parent laws were meant to be obeyed?
[*To* Sc.]   Lead on, sir.   (*To his Mother with cold
courtesy.*)   Madam, — may I trouble you?

· [*He thrusts her gently aside and passes out with the*
Sc.; *the door is shut and fastened from without.*
C.'s M. *rushes to door, which she attempts to force*
without success.

C.'s M.   In vain I batter at a senseless door,
I'll to the keyhole train my tortured ear.
(*Listening.*)   Dead silence! . . . is it over — or,
      to come?
Hark! was not that the click of meeting shears? . . .
Again! and followed by the sullen thud
Of thumbs that drop upon linoleum! . . .

[*The door is opened and* CONRAD *appears, pale but*
erect. N. B. — The whole of this scene has been
compared to one in "La Tosca," which, however,
it exceeds in horror and intensity.

C.'s M.   They send him back to me, bereft of
      both!
My CONRAD! What? — repulse a Mother's Arms!
CON. (*with chilling composure*).   Yes, Madam,
      for between us ever more,
A barrier invisible is raised,
And should I strive to reach those arms again,
Two spectral thumbs would press me coldly back —
The thumbs I sucked in blissful ignorance,
The thumbs that solaced me in solitude,

The thumbs your County Council took from me,
And your endearments scarcely will replace!
Where, Madam, lay the sin in sucking them?
The dog will lick his foot, the cat her claw,
His paws sustain the hibernating bear —
And you decree no law to punish *them!*
Yet, in your rage for infantine reform,
You rushed this most ridiculous enactment —
Its earliest victim — your neglected son!

> C.'s M. (*falling at his feet*).   Say, CONRAD, you
>   will some day pardon me?
> CON. (*bitterly, as he regards his maimed hands.*)
>   Ay — on the day these pollards send forth
>   shoots!

[*His* MOTHER *turns aside with a heartbroken wail;*
    CONRAD *standing apart in gloomy estrangement*
    as the Curtain descends.

www.ingramcontent.com/pod-product-compliance
Lightning Source LLC
Chambersburg PA
CBHW030327270326
41926CB00010B/1530